SMARTGUIDE

CRE▲TIVE
HOMEOWNER®

ceramic tile

step by step

CREATIVE HOMEOWNER®, Upper Saddle River, New Jersey

SMART GUIDE: CERAMIC TILE

MANAGING EDITOR	Fran Donegan
SENIOR GRAPHIC DESIGNER	Glee Barre
EDITORIAL ASSISTANT	Sara Markowitz
PHOTO COORDINATOR	Mary Dolan
INDEXER	Schroeder Indexing Services
DIGITAL IMAGING SPECIALIST	Frank Dyer
SMART GUIDE® SERIES COVER DESIGN	Clarke Barre
FRONT COVER PHOTOGRAPHY	John Parsekian/CH

CREATIVE HOMEOWNER

VICE PRESIDENT AND PUBLISHER	Timothy O. Bakke
ART DIRECTOR	David Geer
MANAGING EDITOR	Fran J. Donegan
PRODUCTION COORDINATOR	Sara M. Markowitz

Current Printing (last digit)
10 9 8 7 6 5 4 3 2

Manufactured in the United States of America

Smart Guide: Ceramic Tile, Second Edition
Library of Congress Control Number: 2009920891
ISBN-10: 1-58011-462-8
ISBN-13: 978-1-58011-462-2

CREATIVE HOMEOWNER®
A Division of Federal Marketing Corp.
24 Park Way
Upper Saddle River, NJ 07458
www.creativehomeowner.com

contents

Chapter 1 **Tile Basics** `6`
• A Short History of Tile • Tile Characteristics • Tile Sizes and Shapes • Trim and Specialty Tiles

Chapter 2 **Tools & Materials** `12`
• Layout and Prep Tools • Cutting Tools • Setting Tools and Materials • Finishing Tools • Basic Materials • Mortar and Adhesives • Grouts and Sealers

Chapter 3 **Tiling Floors** `24`
• Design Basics • Planning the Layout • Preparing the Floor • Reinforcing the Subfloor • Tiling Over Concrete • Establishing Working Lines • Installing Floor Tiles

Chapter 4 **Tiling Walls** `46`
• Design and Layout • Preparing Walls for Tile • Installing New Drywall • Installing Wall Tile

Chapter 5 **Tiling Countertops** `62`
• Planning the Layout • Preparing Countertops • Making a Sink Cutout • Laying the Field Tiles • Partial Tile and Edging • Installing a Backsplash • Finishing a Backsplash

Chapter 6 **Tubs & Showers** `78`
• Preparing the Site • Installing Prefab Pans • Installing a Mortar-Bed Floor • Setting Tub and Shower Tile • Applying Adhesive • Installing Accessories

Chapter 7 **Specialty Tiling** `90`
• Fireplaces • Tiling a Fireplace Face • Stairs • Tiling Existing Concrete • Finishing a Slab

Chapter 8 **Maintenance & Repairs** `100`
• Routine Cleaning • Routine Maintenance • Fixing Broken Tiles • Fixing Trapped Tiles

Glossary `110`

Index `111`

Photo Credits/Metric Conversion `112`

safety first

Though all the designs and methods in this book have been reviewed for safety, it is not possible to overstate the importance of using safe construction methods. What follows are reminders; some do's and don'ts of basic carpentry. They are not substitutes for your own common sense.

- *Always* use caution, care, and good judgment when following the procedures described in this book.

- *Always* be sure that the electrical setup is safe; be sure that no circuit is overloaded and that all power tools and electrical outlets are properly grounded. Do not use power tools in wet locations.

- *Always* read container labels on paints, solvents, and other products; provide ventilation, and observe all other warnings.

- *Always* read the manufacturer's instructions for using a tool, especially the warnings.

- *Always* use hold-downs and push sticks whenever possible when working on a table saw. Avoid working short pieces if you can.

- *Always* remove the key from any drill chuck (portable or press) before starting the drill.

- *Always* pay deliberate attention to how a tool works so that you can avoid being injured.

- *Always* know the limitations of your tools. Do not try to force them to do what they were not designed to do.

- *Always* make sure that any adjustment is locked before proceeding. For example, always check the rip fence on a table saw or the bevel adjustment on a portable saw before starting to work.

- *Always* clamp small pieces firmly to a bench or other work surface when using a power tool on them.

- *Always* wear the appropriate rubber or work gloves when handling chemicals, moving or stacking lumber, or doing heavy construction.

- *Always* wear a disposable face mask when you create dust by sawing or sanding. Use a special filtering respirator when working with toxic substances and solvents.

- *Always* wear eye protection, especially when using power tools or striking metal on metal or concrete; a chip can fly off, for example, when chiseling concrete.

- *Always* be aware that there is seldom enough time for your body's reflexes to save you from injury from a power tool in a dangerous situation; everything happens too fast. Be *alert!*

- *Always* keep your hands away from the business ends of blades, cutters, and bits.

- *Always* hold a circular saw firmly, usually with both hands so that you know where they are.

- *Always* use a drill with an auxiliary handle to control the torque when large-size bits are used.

- *Always* check your local building codes when planning new construction. The codes are intended to protect public safety and should be observed to the letter.

- *Never* work with power tools when you are tired or under the influence of alcohol or drugs.

- *Never* cut tiny pieces of wood or pipe using a power saw. Cut small pieces off larger pieces.

- *Never* change a saw blade or a drill or router bit unless the power cord is unplugged. Do not depend on the switch being off; you might accidentally hit it.

- *Never* work in insufficient lighting.

- *Never* work while wearing loose clothing, hanging hair, open cuffs, or jewelry.

- *Never* work with dull tools. Have them sharpened, or learn how to sharpen them yourself.

- *Never* use a power tool on a work-piece—large or small—that is not firmly supported.

- *Never* saw a workpiece that spans a large distance between horses without close support on each side of the cut; the piece can bend, closing on and jamming the blade, causing saw kickback.

- *Never* support a workpiece from underneath with your leg or other part of your body when sawing.

- *Never* carry sharp or pointed tools, such as utility knives, awls, or chisels, in your pocket. If you want to carry such tools, use a special-purpose tool belt with leather pockets and holders.

introduction

Ceramic tiles have always been used in homes for decoration—and they still are today. Tile is available in an almost endless variety of shapes and colors to suit any house style and any taste. But tile also offers a combination of qualities you won't find in many other building materials. It's extremely durable. It doesn't rot or burn or provide a nesting space or food source for insects. If you install it correctly, tile is one of the few materials that should last as long as your house without a major update or a complete replacement.

Granted, it takes a little longer to install tile than it does to lay down a carpet or slap up a sheet of drywall. But in this book you'll find complete details and step-by-step photos to take you through every type of tile job. You'll get sensible, understandable help with selecting the right materials, using tools safely and effectively, and preparing both existing and new areas for tile jobs that last.

You'll be able to tile kitchens and counters, baths and vanities, floors and walls—using the same techniques as the professionals. And just in case someone drops a heavy pot on your new floor, there's also a section on repairs and maintenance.

chapter 1

tile basics

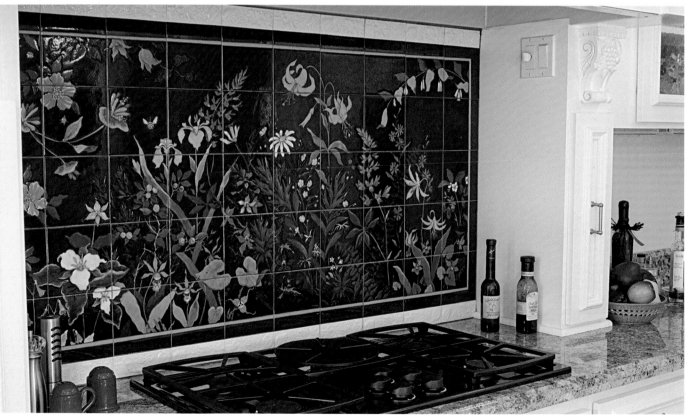

MODERN CERAMIC AND STONE TILES provide hundreds of design options. Unlike many other materials used on floors, walls, and counters, tiles do not burn, fade, or easily stain, although some natural stone tiles must be sealed for protection. Tile resists wear better than most interior materials, and it should last as long as the surfaces that support it.

You don't need to pour a concrete slab to support tile, but you do need to beef up floors, countertops, and other surfaces to make them rigid. Even the slight flexing you generate while walking across a wood floor may crack grout seams. But you can easily increase stiffness by adding a layer of plywood or backer board, or by reinforcing the floor frame itself.

The old-fashioned method of installation, called thickset, required careful trowel work to create a thick, level bed of solid mortar that served as a base for the tile. Using the modern method, called thinset, there is no need for the mortar bed for most applications. You simply rake out adhesive and start embedding your tiles.

A Short History of Tile

The earliest forms of ceramic tile date back to prehistoric times, when the use of clay as a building material was developed independently in several early cultures. The precursors of modern tile were roughly shaped and not nearly as strong as tile today. The material was dug from river banks, roughly formed into building blocks, and baked dry in the sun. The first tiles were crude, but even 6,000 years ago people were decorating them by adding pigments for color and carving low-relief designs into their surfaces.

Firing Tile

The ancient Egyptians were the first to discover that firing clay tiles at high temperatures in a kiln made them stronger and more water-resistant. Many ancient cultures also used thin squares of fired clay as decorative elements in their architecture.

Buildings in ancient Mesopotamian cities were fronted with unglazed terra-cotta and colorful decorative tiles. Ancient Greeks and Romans used ceramics for the floors, roofs, and even the plumbing in their buildings. The Chinese used a white clay called kaolin to develop the white-colored and durable ceramic known as porcelain.

Tiles in medieval Europe were generally reserved for the floors of churches. Across the continent, the Byzantines excelled in using tile at a small scale; they created expressive mosaic patterns and murals using ceramic tile, as well as pieces of glass and stone.

Glazing Tile

Persian ceramicists, inspired by imported Chinese porcelain, created a decorative tradition that spread across

South Asia, North Africa, into Spain with the Moors, and eventually throughout Europe. Because their Islamic religion prohibited using human images in art, artisans turned to brightly colored tiles with ornate and intertwined patterns.

Solid-color glazed tiles were cut and assembled into large-scale mosaics with subtle color gradations. The Islamic artisans also developed metal oxide glazes using tin, copper, cobalt, manganese, and antimony, which made tile glazes more brilliant and durable.

By the fifteenth century, metal oxide-glazed tile had become popular in Italy, and their design influence moved northward with Italian craftsmen. Major European trading centers gave their names to local design motifs and types of tile that are still used, including delft tile (from Delft in Holland), and majolica tile (from Majorca in Spain).

Modern Tile

Today, most commercial tile manufacturers use the pressed-dust method of construction. First, a mixture of ingredients is pressed into the desired tile shape. Then the tile is glazed (or left unglazed) and baked in a kiln. Some tile makers may extrude tile shapes by squeezing them through a press into a die or by rolling them out flat and cutting the tile shapes using a form much like a cookie cutter.

Whatever the method, all ceramic tile must be fired to become durable. The purity of the clay, the number of firings, and the temperature of the kiln determine the quality and price. Kiln temperatures vary from about 900° F to 2,500° F. Lower firing temperatures produce more porous tile and soft glazes; higher temperatures produce dense, nonporous tile and hard glazes.

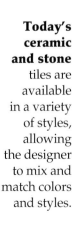

Today's ceramic and stone tiles are available in a variety of styles, allowing the designer to mix and match colors and styles.

Modern ceramic tile allows you to cover different surfaces with a multihued tile that ties a room together.

Tile Characteristics

There are several types of ceramic tile and many ways to categorize them. The built-in properties can make one better than another for a particular installation.

Firing and Glazes

When most tile is first formed it has to dry enough to become stable. The temperature of the kiln determines the porosity of the finish glaze. Tiles fired at lower temperatures generally are more porous and have softer glazes than tiles fired at higher temperatures.

These surface coatings can be used to add color and decoration, and to protect the tile body. Color is commonly included in a mixture of pigments that is added before the tile is fired or applied to a hardened tile and bonded with a second firing. Glazed tiles range from a high-gloss to a dull matte finish.

Water Absorption

There are four basic categories of tile; they are rated by how much water they absorb. More porous tiles are generally softer and absorb more water. They are less expensive, however. Less-porous tiles generally are harder and may be more expensive.

Nonvitreous tile absorbs about 7 percent or more water; semivitreous tile absorbs between 3 percent and 7 percent water; vitreous tile absorbs between 0.6 percent and 3 percent water, and impervious tile absorbs 0.5 percent or less water. Generally, the longer the firing time and the higher the firing temperature, the more nonporous (or vitreous) the tile. Vitreous and impervious tiles include ceramic and glass mosaic varieties, as well as porcelain tiles. Don't use nonvitreous or semivitreous tiles outdoors in cold climates. Water trapped in the tile body will alternately freeze and thaw, cracking the tile.

Tile porosity becomes important in the choice of tiles for wet conditions such as a tub surround because water absorbed by porous tiles can harbor bacteria and eventually penetrate the substrate, loosening the tile bond.

Tile Selection

When you visit your tile dealer, the ceramic tile probably will be divided into basic categories of wall, floor, and ceramic mosaic tile. There are also many specialty tiles, including hand-painted tiles and border strips.

Floor Tiles. Most glazed floor tiles work on countertops and other horizontal surfaces subject to heavy use. Some may be too heavy to set on walls without special supports during the installation, such as a batten board or a row of nails. Some come in sizes up to 24 inches square and may be unwieldy and out of scale as wall tile. Glazed floor tiles often are listed in manufacturers' catalogs as glazed quarry tile or glazed pavers. Generally, you use glazed floor tiles on interior floors only, but some glazed floor tiles have a fine carbide grit incorporated into the glaze to make them slip-resistant in wet areas.

Wall Tiles. Wall tiles generally are thin, lightweight, non-vitreous (porous) tiles coated with a soft glaze. Most don't have the strength to stand up to floor traffic. You also can use sheet tile mounted on a backing of paper, plastic mesh, or fabric mesh. The sheets eliminate the laborious process of spacing individual tiles.

Ceramic Mosaic Tiles. All tiles that are 2 inches square or smaller are considered mosaic tiles. Generally, these dense-bodied vitreous tiles resist water, stains, impact, frost, and abrasion, making them suitable for practically any application. Shapes include squares, rectangles, hexagons, circles, teardrops, clover leafs, and pebble designs, among others. Most ceramic mosaic tiles are mounted on a backing sheet.

Antique Tiles. Although some rare old tiles command very high prices, others are relatively affordable. All are collectible, including Victorian art tiles, Arts and Crafts tiles, and Art Deco tiles, among others. If you can't find the real thing, check with companies specializing in imported hand-painted tiles. Many include a selection of reproduction antique designs.

Hand-Painted and Mural Tiles. Large tile manufacturers offer a broad selection of domestic and imported hand-painted tiles. Several even employ a staff of artists to make personalized hand-painted tiles to order, as do small independent artisans and ceramic shops. Hand-painted tiles are available as individual accents to spruce up a kitchen countertop or fireplace surround.

Some hand-painted tiles have sculptured surfaces, while others are hand-cut into unusual shapes. Custom-made hand-painted tiles vary widely in price—from $20 to over $100 per piece—depending on whether they are chosen from stock designs or are custom-made to your specifications.

If hand-painted tiles are too costly, there are alternatives you can use. Most tile dealers also carry decorator tiles and picture tiles with silk screen or decal designs at a more affordable price.

Ceramic tiles with interlocking patterns can form a centerpiece by themselves or in a surrounding field of tile.

While ancient mosaics were installed piece by piece (left); intricate patterns are now available on full tiles (right).

Larger tiles, trim strips, and accent tiles can be combined into highly decorative and colorful panels.

Tile Sizes and Shapes

Field tiles come in several different shapes, which you can use singly or in various combinations to form patterns. The actual size of these tiles may vary ⅛ inch more or less, as will the thickness, depending on the manufacturer. This means you can't always mix tiles from different manufacturers.

Single Tiles

This is the type of ceramic tile that most do-it-yourselfers use: single tiles laid one at a time. They are available in a great variety of sizes, colors, and patterns. Most custom decorative and hand-painted tiles fall into this category as well. Tiles typically are ¼ to ⅜ inch thick and range in size from 1 × 1 inch to 12 × 12 inches square, although larger sizes and different shapes are available. Most often, layouts work out with a grid of field tiles and at least some partial tiles around the edges. The size you find listed in a manufacturer's catalog generally is nominal and not actual. It generally includes an allowance for grout.

Sheet-Mounted Tiles

Sheet tiles are evenly spaced tiles mounted on a backing sheet of paper, plastic mesh, or fabric mesh. They also may be joined by small dabs of vinyl, polyurethane, or silicone rubber in a process called dot-mounting. Many sheets are 12 inches square or larger. It's wise to use sheet-mounted applications of small tiles that would be very time-consuming to set one by one. Small sizes on sheets provide the option of laying tiles on gentle curves. For the most part, the sheets are installed the same way that individual tiles are installed. All sheet-mounted tiles require grouting. And you can cut the backing to install partial sheets.

Pregrouted Tile Panels

Eliminating the need to grout joints sounds like a good idea. And some tile outlets may offer pregrouted tile panels to do the job. But the grout is actually a flexible polyurethane, polyvinyl chloride, rubber grout, or silicone caulk. Without rigid grout between tiles, these sheets often are flexible enough to bend and stretch with normal building movement. A variety of trim pieces generally are available to complete the installation. You use tubes of matching silicone caulk to grout the joints between panel edges and trim pieces. Typically, the grout is treated with a special mildew and fungus inhibitor, making these panels suitable for shower and tub enclosures. Because of this chemical treatment, the Food and Drug Administration does not recommend installing the sheets on kitchen countertops or on other serving and food-preparation areas. These flexible grouts typically are available in white and a wide range of colors.

Trim and Specialty Tiles

All tiles that are not field tiles are referred to as trim tiles. They are used to create smooth, finished edges and corners for specific areas. In tile catalogs, manufacturers usually picture the available sizes and shapes of trim pieces for different tiles in their line.

- **Angles.** These tiles include inside and outside corners that create sharp turns instead of rounded edges.
- **Aprons.** Half-size tiles called aprons are used to fill in narrow areas, such as along the front of a countertop.
- **Bases.** Tiles designed specifically for the floor line, called base trims or runners, have a finished top edge. They are used in areas where the floor has been tiled but the wall has not.
- **Beads.** These trims are sometimes called quarter-rounds, and are used to finish off corners and edges. The narrow pieces turn a rounded, 90-degree angle.
- **Bullnose.** These are regular field tiles with one curved and finished edge. They neatly trim a course of tile that ends without turning a corner. Often, a bullnose tile is paired with an apron tile meeting the bullnose at a right angle. The result is a smoothly turned corner and edge. There are surface bullnose tiles designed for thinset installations and radiused bullnose designed for thicker, mortar-bed installations.
- **Countertop Trims.** These trim pieces are set on the outside edge of a countertop. The raised lip is designed to prevent drips. Many V-cap tiles have this feature.
- **Coves.** These pieces are used to gently turn corners at a right angle. The corner can turn either inward or outward. Cove base turns a corner at floor level. Special cove pieces that have a finished edge turn a corner at the top row of a backsplash. Other cove pieces do not have finished edges.
- **Miters.** Two miter pieces together form a corner separated by a grout joint.
- **Rounds.** These trim tiles create a rounded corner instead of an angular one.
- **Swimming-Pool Edging.** These tiles are designed to cover the coping on swimming pools. They require a thickset mortar bed.
- **V-caps.** Although they are called V-shaped, these edging tiles often are more L-shaped to cover the perimeter of a counter, for example, and wrap around the front edge of plywood and backer board.
- **Windowsill Trim.** Windowsill tile has a finished edge on one side and a rounded corner on the other. It covers the sill itself and turns to meet the tile on the wall. Without this trim piece, you would need two tiles: a flat field tile for the sill itself and a quarter-round to turn the corner. Sill trim simplifies the installation.

4¼" Octagon

1⅜" x 1⅜" Spot

1" x 1"

2" x 2"

4¼" x 4¼"

6" x 6"

10" x 10"

12" x 12"

1" x 2"

2" x 4"

4" x 6"

4" x 8"

1" Hexagon

2" Hexagon

5" Hexagon

6" Hexagon

8" Hexagon

6" Ogee

Exploded-View Seam

Standard Grout Seam

Floor Tiles

A—bullnose
B—field tile
C—cove
D—bullnose out-corner
E—field out-corner
F—cove out-corner
G—bullnose in-corner (mitered)
H—field (mitered)
I—cove in-corner
J—bullnose corner
K—bullnose
L—cove end

chapter 2
tools & materials

IF YOU ARE AN ACTIVE DO-IT-YOURSELFER, you probably own most of the tools you'll need for tile work. You may want to buy a few specialized tile tools, such as a wet saw, but you can also rent them. If you are in the process of accumulating how-to tools, consider these general buying guidelines. They can help you collect practical products for all kinds of projects.

Durability. Buy better quality in tools you'll use often, such as a hammer and a saw. Don't pay for heavy-duty contractor tools you'll use occasionally.

Precision. Buy tools that are in the ballpark of your skill level, with features you can really use. Stick with basic tools designed to do one job well. Avoid multipurpose gimmick tools.

Strength. Look for hammers, wrenches, and pry bars that are drop-forged instead of cast metal. Casting traps air bubbles in molten metal, creating weak spots.

Price. If in doubt, avoid the most- and least-expensive models. The top end often has more capacity than you need, and the bottom end often has fundamental flaws.

A—rubber gloves; **B**—work gloves; **C**—knee pads; **D**—safety glasses; **E**—safety goggles; **F**—particle mask; **G**—respirator; **H**—ear protectors

Layout and Prep Tools

You may already have most of the tools needed to lay out a tile project. To square up and level the job, you'll use a level and a square, of course, but you'll also need a chalk-line box to snap guidelines. Where measuring is concerned, take your pick: a measuring tape or a folding carpenter's rule. Not much hammering is involved in tile work, but you may need a hammer (and many other basic tools) to prepare the site—for example, if you have to lay new plywood subflooring. The more prep work you need to do, the more tools you'll need, including a few that will never touch a tile, such as a pipe wrench to loosen fittings in a kitchen or bath.

Remember that tile is hard, and chips can fly when you cut it. Wear safety glasses or goggles to protect your eyes. Because most cutting and grinding procedures create fine dust that can irritate your lungs, wear a respirator or at least a mask. You may also want to invest in a set of knee pads, particularly if you are planning to tile a floor.

A—portable drill; **B**—level; **C**—circular saw; **D**—framing square; **E**—pipe wrench; **F**—backer board cutting tool; **G**—chalk-line box; **H**—combination square; **I**—6-in. drywall taping knife; **J**—measuring tape; **K**—hammer; **L**—utility knife; **M**—sandpaper; **N**—masonry chisel; **O**—carpenter's pencil; **P**—screwdriver **Q**—putty knife; **R**—utility saw

Cutting Tools

To make straight cuts in glazed tile, all you need is a conventional glass cutter, a metal straightedge, and a length of coat-hanger wire or thin dowel. Simply score the glazed surface of the tile with the cutter guided along the straightedge. Then place the tile on the wire or dowel with the score mark centered directly above it, and press down on both sides of the tile to snap it.

But there are a few improvements that you can easily make on this somewhat simple approach. The most basic is using a cutter called a snap tile cutter because the tool scores and snaps tile. If you have many straight cuts to make, a snap cutter will speed things along considerably and produce cleaner cuts. (Snap cutters are available at tool-rental shops.)

These tools come in several sizes and variations, but most consist of a metal frame that holds the tile in position and a carbide-tipped blade or wheel that travels along a guide rod, ensuring a square cut. Most also have a built-in ridge and a handle that you use to snap the tile once it's scored. After positioning the tile, draw the carbide blade or wheel across the surface to score it. Then press down on the handle until the tile snaps. (See "Using a Snap Tile Cutter," opposite.)

Most snap cutters will not work on large, thick tiles, such as quarry tile or pavers. If you have just a few of these tiles to cut, use this variation of the score-and-snap method. Fit a hacksaw with a carbide-grit blade; then cut a groove about 1/16 inch deep in the face of the tile. (Very thick tiles may require a second cut on the back to get a clean snap.) Then set the tile over a wood dowel or heavy wire, and press down sharply to snap. This system will work but should be reserved for only one or two problem cuts. If you have many tiles proving troublesome to cut in a snap cutter, use a wet saw.

This tool is also the best bet (on any kind of tile) if you have many irregular cuts to make. A wet saw is basically a stationary circular saw with a water-cooled carbide-grit blade. (You can rent one for the job at a tool-rental shop.) The saw component stays put, and you guide the tile into it on a sliding table.

A—wet saw; **B**—cordless drill with carbide hole saw; **C**—handheld grinder with carbide bit; **D**—snap tile cutter; **E**—tile nippers; **F**—glass cutter; **G**—hacksaw with carbide blade

Using a Snap Tile Cutter

The handle on a typical snap cutter has two functions. First use it to score the tile. Then press down to split the tile along the score line.

A snap cutter makes quick work of square cuts. Position the tile against the stop at the head of the tool, and draw the scoring wheel across the surface.

Using a Wet Saw

1. A typical wet saw comes fitted to a water reservoir. A circulating system feeds a stream of water onto the cutting area to lubricate the blade.

2. On a wet saw, you feed the work into the blade instead of pulling the blade into the work. You need to hold the tile securely on the cutting table.

3. The fine-toothed blade slices through tile more slowly than a wood blade cuts through lumber. The saw can handle coves and other shapes.

TILE TIP: Be sure to wear safety glasses when using a wet saw. Also pay particular attention to how you feed the tile into the blade. The tile should be firmly seated on the platform, and you should ease it into the blade, making sure that your fingers stay clear.

Cutting Irregular Shapes

There are bound to be spots where you can't use a full tile or a partial tile trimmed using a snap cutter. In some cases, you can get by using a straight-cutting tool to slice off a corner. For example, if you are tiling near a baseboard convector, you may be able to avoid a feed pipe coming through the floor by trimming off a corner of a tile with a snap cutter. The tile may not close up neatly around the pipe, but that won't matter if the cut is concealed by the convector cover.

In many cases, a tile nipper will do the job. (See "Using Tile Nippers," below.) The trick is to be patient and take small bites, sometimes as small as ⅛ inch. Once you get the knack of nibbling away at tiles without cracking them, you'll find that it doesn't take long to fit a tile against a pipe.

Where a pipe will protrude through a tile, instead of nicking its edge, another option is to fit your power drill with a masonry hole saw—a tubular bit with cutting teeth. It's wise to test out a hole saw cut on scrap tile. You need to hold the drill steady and keep the bit plumb, particularly as you start the cut. The result is a neat hole that allows for grout or caulk to be applied between the tile and pipe. Of course, this approach will work only if you can cut or disconnect the pipe in order to slip the tile in position.

You can also use a wet saw to make irregular cutouts. This tool is particularly handy if you need to fit a tile against molding or any surface with an intricate shape. The idea is to make a series of closely spaced parallel cuts to the required depths. Then break out the thin slices of tile standing between saw kerfs.

Using Tile Nippers

1. Start your cuts by taking very small bites along the edge of the tile. You should work up to your cut marks gradually, which takes patience.

2. You can take slightly larger bites once the area is more defined. It pays to practice on some scrap tiles—and plan for extra waste just in case.

3. The teeth of a nipper will leave a slightly ragged edge. Where appearance counts, you may want to clean up the nipped edges using a file.

TILE TIP: If you haven't used this tool before, expect to break a few tiles before you get the hang of it. If you need to fit a tile around part of a pipe or other obstruction, first mark your cut line. Then start taking very small bites with the teeth of the nipper.

Setting Tools and Materials

To set tile, you'll need tools for mixing and spreading adhesive and for embedding and leveling the tiles. You will also need a way to maintain even grout lines. Wall tiles often have spacing nubs molded into their sides. Old-timers sometimes used cotton cord to establish uniform spacing for floor tiles. Some pros are so experienced that they can do the job by eye. But most do-it-yourselfers will find it useful to use plastic spacers to place between the tiles.

Mixing and Spreading Adhesive

You should use premixed adhesive on thinset work, and mix your own only in special cases. If you are tackling a thickset mortar job and mixing large amounts of cement-based adhesive, you will need a mason's hoe and wheelbarrow or a large sheet-metal cement-mixing barge. To mix powdered grout, use a bucket and a mortar-mixing paddle or paint mixer chucked in an electric drill. (Use the mixer at a slow speed, 300 rpm or less.)

In most cases, a notched trowel is all you need to apply adhesive. Typically, only one side and one end of the trowel is notched. This allows you to use the flat side to spread the adhesive initially and the notched side to comb out the mix and create even ribs.

Trowels come with various-size square or V-shaped notches for spreading different adhesives for different tiles. Choose trowels for your project based on the size of the notches. The size is specified by the tile or adhesive manufacturer and is usually listed on the packaging of the adhesive. You may need other mason's tools, such as floats, to level and finish thickset mortar beds.

Spreading Adhesive

1. Spread adhesive on one section of the floor at a time, not the entire surface, to give yourself some working room on the subfloor surface.

2. Trowel notches produce evenly spaced ribs of adhesive that are the same size. Embed the tiles in the ribs with a slight twist for a secure bond.

3. You can use a sweeping stroke over large areas. First spread out a pile of adhesive before creating the ridges using the toothed edge.

TILE TIP: Using a notched trowel makes it easy to spread adhesive. You can sweep the blade back and forth and be certain that you are leaving the right amount of adhesive. The notches should match the recommendation of the adhesive manufacturer.

Tile Spacers

To ensure even spacing for grout joints, some tiles (typically wall tiles) have small spacing nubs molded into the edges. When you set two of these tiles together, the nubs match up and create a gap for grout. If the tiles you are using do not have nubs, there are several ways to keep an even layout.

The most reliable system is to set molded plastic spacers in the gaps. These cross-shaped fittings are available in many sizes (generally from 1/32 to 1/2 inch), so you can use them on small tiles with narrow grout lines and on large tiles with thick grout lines.

Follow the tile manufacturer's recommendations about which size and type to use. Some can be set flat, left in place, and grouted over. Many are set vertically and removed after the tile sets but before you grout.

On countertops, you can mark the centers of the grout lines, attach 6d finishing nails at each end, and stretch dampened cotton cord between them. On floors with wide grout joints, you may want to use wooden battens as spacers.

Embedding and Leveling Tiles

To assist in bedding tiles into adhesive, you may want to use a hammer or rubber mallet and a bedding block. To make a bedding block, cut a wood block large enough to cover several tiles at once, and cover it with heavy fabric or scrap carpet. You may need a metal straightedge to periodically make sure that the tiles are even and level and that the grout joints remain aligned.

Embedding Tiles

1. Moderate pressure combined with a slight side-to-side motion is usually enough to bond the tile with the adhesive.

2. Small plastic spacers help to maintain even grout seams as you work tiles into position. You usually remove spacers before grouting.

3. Use a piece of 2×4 wrapped in a carpet scrap to even out the tile surface, if necessary. Gentle blows with a hammer provide enough force.

TILE TIP: You need only moderate pressure over ribs of tile adhesive to create a good bond. But tapping on a padded block that reaches over several tiles may be necessary to be sure that the tiles are flush.

A—masonry trowel; B—sponge; C—grout sealer with applicator; D—bucket; E—grout float; F—grout bag; G—rubber mallet; H—scouring pad; I—bedding block; J—tile spacers; K—notched trowel; L—carbide emery cloth; M—grout saw; N—caulking gun; O—spacer remover

Finishing Tools

Grout Tools

To apply grout, the typical procedure is to spread a liberal amount across the tile surface, working on a diagonal to the joints using a rubber float or squeegee. With repeated passes you gradually force grout into the joints and compact it.

You can also use a grout bag. It's similar to a pastry bag and has a small fitting on one end to which you can attach nozzles of different sizes to control the amount of grout applied to the joint. After filling the bag, squeeze it to lay a bead of grout directly into the joint. Grout bags work well in situations where cleaning excess grout off the tile surface would be difficult, or where the grout might stain the tile surface.

Drawbacks to using the bag include problems with applying a fast-setting grout and mixing this grout to a usable consistency. If the grout is too thin and watery, it won't bond well. If you use the more common method of grouting with a float, it may help if you use a squeegee to clear excess grout off the surface. Then, as the grout dries, you'll need a good sponge or two to remove the grout haze. Rinse the sponge regularly in clean water, and make several passes.

Striking and Jointing Tools

Although most grout is left flush (or nearly flush) to make tile surfaces easier to clean, you may want to strike the grout joints to create a particular pattern. You can buy special striking tools or simply run down the joints using a wooden stick or small tool handle.

Finally, you may need a caulking gun to install polyurethane or silicone caulk in joints where the tile meets dissimilar materials—for example, where wall tiles meet the rim of a tub. Just insert the caulking tube into the gun, snip the tip of the caulking tube, and apply pressure on the gun trigger to fill the gap.

Basic Materials

Although ceramic tile can be laid over a variety of existing surfaces, there may be cases when you must install a smooth, rigid surface.

Cement Backer Board

Also called cementitious backer units, or CBUs, cement backer board is a rigid, portland cement-based panel designed for use as a substrate or underlayment for ceramic tile in wet or dry areas. Sometimes the binder material is made of fiberglass-reinforced coatings. Different types are recommended for interior floors, interior walls, and exterior walls.

Next to a thick-bed mortar installation, cement backer board is the best substrate for wet areas. Although it is not waterproof, water will not damage it. Wood, plywood, particleboard, and drywall underlayments will deteriorate when exposed to water. And because cement backer board is a rigid, dense, dimensionally stable product, it does not expand and contract as much as conventional wood subflooring and underlayment materials.

Backer board is available in several thicknesses. The most commonly used is ½-inch thick. The panels also come in several widths, but are usually 4 × 4 or 3 × 5 feet.

You install CBUs basically the same way you install drywall. The panels are a bit trickier to cut, but you can score and snap the panels to get a clean edge. Because CBUs are heavy and rigid, install them directly over wall studs using corrosion-resistant nails or screws.

Backer board is also fireproof, so you can use it in place of asbestos board as an insulating material for woodstove surrounds. And using it in conjunction with tile may allow reduced clearances between the stove and wall. Check the manufacturer's directions and local building codes to be sure of clearances at combustion sources.

A—thinset mortar mix; **B**—premixed tile grouts; **C**—cement backer board; **D**—plywood; **E**—greenboard; **F**—tile mastic; **G**—tile and grout sealer; **H**—tile and grout cleaner; **I**—fiberglass mesh tape; **J**—galvanized screws; **K**—caulking products; **L**—4-mil plastic film (waterproof membrane)

Thickset

- Tile and Grout
- ¼" Adhesive
- 1" Mortar Bed
- Reinforcing Wire
- ¾" T+G Subfloor
- 2x8 Floor Joist

Thinset

- Tile and Grout
- Thinset Adhesive
- ¾" Plywood Substrate
- ½" Plywood Subfloor
- 2x8 Floor Joist

Mortar and Adhesives

The traditional setting method is to lay the tiles directly in a bed of wet portland cement mortar. It's still used in some situations—for example, if you need to create a sloping floor in a shower enclosure. But most tile work is done using thinset adhesive.

Thickset

Installing thick-bed mortar requires considerable experience. Some tile-setters lay down the mortar bed, smooth it, allow it to cure, and then set the tiles over the bed with a bond coat of cement adhesive. In any case, the job is best left to a professional.

Thinset

There are many thinset adhesives on the market. A tile dealer can recommend the best adhesive for the job, but you will probably wind up using a cement-based adhesive (mortar) or an organic mastic adhesive, and in some cases an epoxy-based mortar.

Portland Cement Mortars

These adhesives are actually forms of cement-based mortar, although they should not be confused with the portland cement mortar used for thick-bed installations. Most of these nonflammable, thinset mortars come in powder form. Some must be mixed with sand before use.

Some come as premixed liquids. Powdered forms are mixed with water or a liquid latex additive.

Dry-Set Mortars

These are the most common adhesives, generally sold in powder form and mixed with water. Highly resistant to impact, dry-set mortar can be cleaned up easily with water. Once cured, this mortar is not affected by prolonged contact with water, so it can be used in wet installations.

A typical installation has a layer about ³⁄₃₂ inch thick. The material will cover and level minor surface irregularities, but it is not intended as a setting bed or for leveling very rough surfaces.

Dry-set mortars adhere well to a variety of substrate materials, including relatively smooth masonry, insulation board, drywall, and cement backer board. Some types are suitable for use over plywood. Check the label for appropriate applications.

Latex Portland Cement Mortars

These mortars are a mixture of portland cement, sand, and a liquid latex additive. They have the same basic applications as dry-set mortars, although they have higher compressive and bond strengths and greater flexibility.

Latex portland cement mortars cost a bit more than the dry-set kind, but they perform better.

Organic Mastic Adhesives

Although most of these adhesives do not have the bond strength or leveling properties of thinsets, they are the easiest to apply. Most brands cannot be used in wet installations or near heat sources, however. (Organic adhesives generally should not be used in areas with temperatures over 140 degrees F.) Suitable backings include drywall, smooth plaster or mortar, plywood, tile backer board, and smooth, dry concrete. Organic mastics are water-based.

Epoxy-Based Mortars

Epoxies are not used much by do-it-yourselfers because they are more expensive and harder to apply than other adhesives. You must mix the resin and hardener to exact proportions and apply them at the correct temperature to ensure the right setting time and pot life. Epoxy mortars are useful when you need a high degree of bond strength or when the tiled surface will receive a high degree of physical or chemical wear. They will adhere to just about any substrate material.

Grouts and Sealers

Grouts

Tile grouts fall into two basic categories: cement-based grout and epoxy grout. Don't confuse grouts used for tiling with caulks, which are used for filling gaps between building materials. For example, silicone caulk is used at joints where tile meets other surfaces. And because silicone is highly flexible, you can use it instead of grout at tiled corners and edges where movement in the substructure would crack ordinary grout joints. It's also good practice to caulk the joint between wall tiles and a tub.

Cement-Based Grouts. These grouts have a base of portland cement, but they differ in the types of additives they contain. Coloring pigments are available for many of them, although precolored grouts also are sold.

Most cement-based grouts come in powdered form to which water or liquid latex is added. Some grouts are premixed and ready to use, but they are usually the most expensive as well. Cement-based grouts include commercial portland cement, dry-set, and latex portland cement grouts.

Portland Cement Grout. A mixture of portland cement and other ingredients, this grout produces a dense, uniformly colored material. Like all cement-based mortars, it is resistant to water but not completely waterproof or stainproof, so it generally requires a sealer. Commercial portland cement grouts are formulated for use with thick-bed portland cement mortar installations. With these, you need to soak the tiles in water before application. These grouts also require damp-curing to prevent shrinking and cracking.

Sealing Grout

Glazed tiles have great resistance to dirt, mold, and mildew. But the grout between tiles can become a chronic cleaning problem unless you protect it with a sealer. Mildew can be removed using bleach. Ground-in dirt on floors and such may be impossible to remove. Here you should use dark grouts.

General cleaning may not take care of stains in grout. Try to scrub the grout using a brush (even an old toothbrush) with a concentrated cleaner and/or bleach.

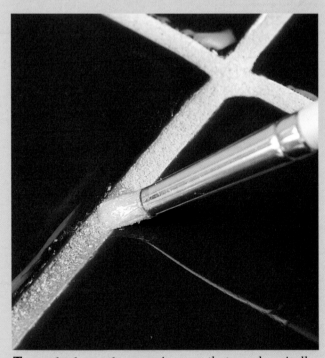

To protect grout seams in areas that are chronically damp or exposed to traffic, use a small brush to coat cleaned grout with a liberal coat of liquid silicone sealer.

Dry-Set Grout. This type of portland cement grout contains additives that increase water-retention. They allow you to grout tiles without presoaking them and without damp-curing the grout once applied. If you are grouting the tiles on a hot, dry day, the grout might dry out so quickly that it will shrink, requiring you to presoak tiles and damp-cure the grout joints anyway.

Latex Portland Cement Grout. This can be any of the preceding grout types that have been mixed with powdered latex and water, or with liquid latex instead of water. This versatile grout is somewhat stronger and more flexible than latex cement mortar.

Epoxy Grout. This grout contains an epoxy resin and hardener, giving it a high degree of chemical resistance, bond strength, and impact resistance. It is the most expensive grout, and therefore usually confined to commercial applications where chemical resistance is required. Epoxy grout generally flows more easily than standard grout and is somewhat more difficult to apply. If your tiles are more than ½ inch thick and the grout joints are less than ¼ inch wide, the grout may not penetrate.

Sealers

Clear liquid tile and grout sealers provide protection against stains and, to some extent, against water penetration at grout joints. Their application is the final step in tile installation. Although glazed tiles themselves do not require a sealer, the cement-based grout joints usually do because they are more porous than tile. Most sealers have a silicone, lacquer, or acrylic base. Different formulations are available for different types of tile and grout in various applications. Sealers generally require reapplication every one to two years to maintain protection. But the extra effort is worth it because they can reduce the formation of mold and mildew in grouted joints.

Grout Types

Tile/Application	Commercial Portland Cement		Sand Portland Cement	Dry-Set	Latex Portland Cement	Epoxy (2, 3)	Silicone or Urethane	Modified Epoxy Emulsion
	Walls	Floors	Walls & Floors	Walls & Floors	(1)		(4)	(1, 3)
Glazed Wall Tile (More than 7% absorption)	✔			✔	✔		✔	
Ceramic Mosaic Tile	✔	✔	✔	✔	✔	✔	✔	✔
Quarry, Paver, and Packing House Tile	✔	✔	✔			✔		✔
Dry or Limited Water Exposure	✔	✔	✔	✔	✔	✔	✔	✔
Wet Areas	✔	✔	✔	✔	✔	✔	✔	✔
Exteriors	✔	✔	✔	✔	✔(5)	✔(5)		✔(5)
Stain Resistance (6)	D	C	E	D	B	A	A	B
Crack Resistance (6)	D	D	E	D	C	B	A Flexible	C
Colorability (6)	B	B	C	B	B	B	Restricted	B

(1) Special cleaning procedures and materials needed.
(2) Mainly used for chemical-resistant properties.
(3) Epoxies are recommended for prolonged temperatures up to 140°F, high-temperature-resistant epoxies up to 350°F.
(4) Special tools needed for proper application. Silicone and urethane are used when installing pregrouted ceramic tile sheets. Silicone grout should not be used on kitchen countertops or other food-preparation surfaces.
(5) Follow manufacturer's directions.
(6) Five performance ratings—best to minimal (A B C D E).

tiling floors

ON FLOORS, ceramic and stone tiles provide a durable surface that will complement practically any room and its furnishings. Bear in mind, though, that tile can be hard and cold underfoot. That's why it is not often used in bedrooms or living rooms, and reserved mainly for kitchens, baths, and entry halls.

Before you lay a ceramic or stone tile floor, the existing floor must be strong and rigid enough to support the added weight of the tile. Strength is rarely a problem because residential floors generally are built to carry at least 40 pounds per square foot—more than enough to carry tile. But you may need to strengthen joists or add extra subflooring (or both) to make the floor rigid enough that it does not flex.

The work area must also be reasonably square for the installation to look good. There are extreme cases (mainly in older homes) where a floor covering with a nondirectional pattern such as carpeting might look better than a grid pattern of tile. But you usually can deal with minor discrepancies by adjusting the tile layout to visually de-emphasize the condition.

Design Basics

Although the subject of design involves numerous considerations—and is largely a matter of personal taste—a few basic principles always apply.

When choosing a tile for your floor, you need to consider five elements: size, shape, color, texture, and pattern. Together, all five elements determine the overall visual effect you are trying to achieve. The first four elements apply to the tile you select. The last element, pattern, is controlled both by the material itself and by the way the tiles are arranged on the floor.

Size

As a general rule, tile size has an inverse effect on rooms: small tiles make a floor look larger, and large tiles make a floor look smaller. If you're tiling a small lavatory with several twists and turns in the walls, a small, simple, and uniform tile will probably look best. If you're tiling a somewhat cavernous entry hall at the foot of a expansive two-story stairwell, 12 × 12-inch tiles may help to pull the large space together.

But there is always a trade-off in design decisions. Where tile size is concerned, it involves both installation time and possible future maintenance. Because large tiles cover a lot of area, installing them is faster than it would be with small tiles. Also, there are fewer grout lines in a field of large tiles, which means less cleaning and sealing as the floor is subjected to daily wear and tear.

Shape

Because most tiles are square, this is the shape people expect to see. When you choose a different shape (hexagonal, octagonal, or ogee, for instance) or combine shapes, such as squares and rectangles, you immediately draw attention to the floor.

Color

Dark colors tend to make a space look smaller, while lighter shades generally provide a more spacious feeling. Warm terra-cotta colors suggest a rustic look, whereas black, white, and bold colors can impart a more modern appearance. Light pastels, such as pink, peach, or light blues and greens, can soften a room while lending an airy feeling. Sharply contrasting colors and patterns usually draw attention to the floor, whereas a single-color or low-contrast color scheme creates a subtle backdrop for furniture or other focal points in the room. You need to plan color schemes carefully, considering wall paint color, natural light, and other factors, to avoid conflicts with other elements in the room.

Texture

The surface texture of a tile often plays a more subtle role than the other style elements. But it is an important link to the overall feeling of a room with a tiled floor. For example, handmade Mexican pavers have an uneven surface that creates a purposefully irregular, heavily textured look. Combined with color gradations within each tile, this can set a distinctly rustic style. On the other hand, machine-made pavers with a uniformly smooth surface texture and even coloring have a crisp, clean look. A highly glazed surface can seem to expand a space and brighten a room, while a matte finish often diminishes space and makes a room feel more cozy.

Tile shapes (and different surface textures) can be combined to create borders and define areas.

Tile patterns range from a subtle contrasting shade in a border to highly defined murals and mosaics.

You can combine tiles of different colors, sizes, patterns, and textures into a unique design.

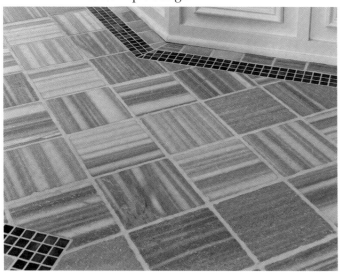

Pattern

The way you combine the different design elements of shape, size, and color determines the overall pattern of the floor. Consider that the pattern serves not only to add visual interest to the floor but also can underscore particular features of a room, such as its length. A strong directional pattern running lengthwise makes a room look longer and narrower, while a crossing pattern makes a room look shorter and wider. You can also use multiple patterns to define areas. For example, you might change a square grid layout in the main field into a diagonal pattern around the edge of a room or along a walkway. A pattern change can also separate spaces—at a pass-through between rooms, for example—while a continuing grid serves to draw them together. Manipulating lines of sight can also increase apparent space and create a unifying effect—for instance, when you continue tile from inside onto an outdoor patio. Generally, busy patterns decrease apparent floor size, while simple patterns enlarge it.

Grout Has an Impact on the Design. Using a contrasting grout color will emphasize a pattern, while a matching grout color provides a more subtle effect. Remember that dark grout hides dirt better than a light color, so think twice before using white grout. If you also plan on tiling the wall, it is usually best to use one size of tile on the wall and another on the floor.

Changing scale or pattern—installing what amounts to a tile baseboard, for example—will separate wall and floor grids and disguise any discrepancies where grout joints might not align. There are many types of specially shaped tiles, generally with a cove shape, that suit this purpose. Also, you can include a strip of border tiles of a contrasting color or pattern around the room perimeter to frame a pattern in the main tile field. Be sure to subtract the thickness of the cove when planning the floor's layout.

Even within these basic guidelines, there are so many possibilities that it pays to experiment before you decide on a final combination of elements. You can do this on your own with graph paper and colored pencils, or use the computer-imaging services available at some tile stores and home centers.

Finish

For indoor floors, you can use a glazed or unglazed tile. Glazed tiles are easier to clean, while some unglazed tiles require sealing and waxing. If you want to use an unglazed tile indoors, use a vitreous quarry tile that is at least somewhat stain resistant. In wet areas, choose a tile with a slip-resistant surface, and avoid slick, highly glazed tiles. Outdoors, unglazed tiles are often a better choice than glazed tiles, which can be slick when wet.

Also, consider investing some extra time in the job of finishing the grout, particularly in damp areas where mildew forms easily on the surface. A protective coat of grout sealer makes cleaning much easier.

Tile color can be uniform but still vary slightly to provide highlights and tie together a large entry area.

Preparing the Floor

Tiling is no different from other do-it-yourself projects in one important respect: much of the work involved (and often the key to a successful project) lies in the preparation. The main concern, of course, is strength. To support tile and grout without flexing enough to cause cracking, the floor must be stronger than a typical floor. It can't flex. This can make a tile floor somewhat less comfortable than a wood floor.

You can install ceramic tile directly over many existing floor coverings if the floor covering itself and the subflooring and framing below are sound. If the existing floor meets these requirements—for example, the plywood floor under carpeting—thoroughly clean the floor and,

if necessary, roughen the existing surface with sandpaper to ensure a good adhesive bond. It's also a good idea to check the surface for raised seams and popped nailheads. You can reduce the seams with a block plane. You can deal with the popped nails in one of two ways: drive them home, or better yet, pull them out and drive screws instead.

The added thickness of tile will cause a change of floor level, which will have to be dealt with at entryways where the tile meets other floor coverings. You may have to trim narrow strips off the bottoms of doors as well.

In many cases, an existing floor structure will require some tear-out and rebuilding. In some houses, you may have to remove the surface flooring, strip some of the subflooring, build up some of the framing, and start from

To support heavy tiles and prevent cracking, you generally need extra subflooring and sometimes extra framing, too.

scratch. In many cases, adding one extra layer of plywood will increase the strength adequately.

If you find that it is too difficult to remove an old floor covering, and it is in bad shape, you may be able to bury it under plywood or a backer-board underlayment and make a sound surface for new tile.

New Construction

If you are working with new floor construction, plan the job to provide extra-strength framing and subflooring for tiled areas. If a standard floor in the house has 2×8s covered with ½-inch plywood sheathing, there are two approaches you could take to build in extra strength: increase the joist size or decrease the joist spacing. You could switch to 2×10s or, if there is not enough room for the extra depth, decrease the spacing between joist centers from the standard 16 inches to 12 inches.

As for subflooring, you could leave the existing ½-inch panels in place and cover them with another layer of ½- or ⅝- or even ¾-inch-thick plywood. There are also special-order floor systems that provide exceptional strength. These include I-beam wood joists, and 1-inch-thick plywood panels milled with overlapping edges. It generally pays to install the plywood using screws instead of nails; they provide more holding power.

If you install an extra layer of subflooring (as most jobs require either extra plywood or cement-based backer board), avoid aligning seams with the existing material. Joints between panels on the different layers should bear on different floor joists.

Strengthening the Subfloor

1. An extra layer of plywood (generally ½ in. thick or more) solidifies the floor. Screws provide more holding power than nails in old and new layers.

2. Locate a weak or sagging joist by checking across several joists using a level. It will rock over the lowest one where the floor dips.

3. Strengthen a weak joist (after propping it up if need be) by adding a second joist secured with construction adhesive and screws.

TILE TIP: Remember that wooden floors are resilient; they flex a bit when you walk on them. But to support tile without cracking, you need to eliminate the flexing as much as possible.

Reinforcing the Subfloor

If an existing floor feels spongy or excessively flexible when you walk on it—or if it squeaks over a large area—chances are that you will need to reinforce it. If the floor sags noticeably, you will need to level it.

Start by renailing or screwing the subfloor to the floor joists. If you have an older, board-type subfloor, you can shim individual loose boards with shingles. Gently tap shims into the space between the joists and the subfloor to prevent movement. Do not drive the shims too force-fully, or they will cause the boards to rise, resulting in a wavy floor. Then nail or screw the boards to the joists.

If several boards are loose or a sagging joist has cre-ated a springy spot in a plywood subfloor, you can add a cleat beside or between the joists in question. For exam-ple, you can cut a short piece of wood the same depth as the joists, coat its top with construction adhesive, tap it into place between joists (under the weak area), and nail it securely.

If a large area of the entire subfloor is weak because joists have settled or shifted, one approach is to strengthen the floor by adding wood or metal bridging. You can also double up weak joists after propping them up temporarily with posts.

Make sure the existing subfloor material itself is in good shape. It should be sound, even, and level. In bath-rooms especially, water damage to the subfloor might not be apparent until you remove the finish flooring. Replace all rotted or water-damaged wood. If a subfloor is simply wet but still sound, allow it to dry thoroughly before tiling over it. Fix the problem causing the wetness to prevent future problems.

Typically, the total thickness of the subfloor, underlay-ment, and existing floor material (if retained) should be at least 1⅛ inches thick. If it is not, build up the subfloor by adding an additional layer of exterior plywood (CDX or better grade), or use cement-based backer board. It is recommended for wet areas. Do not use interior-grade plywood, particleboard, or hardboard.

Underlayment

You will also need to install an underlayment of plywood or backer board over wood-board subfloors, because

Bridging

Bridging is short blocks of wood or strips of metal set between floor joists. It connects the joists to each other and can prevent twisting where the bottom edges are left exposed—for example, over a crawl space. There are two basic types of bridging: wood and metal. Wood bridging can be solid pieces of lumber set perpendicularly between the joists, or smaller pieces of lumber set in an X-shape. Metal bridging uses two strips of steel in an X pattern. Although bridging may not be required by building codes in your floor, most people find that it adds a noticeable degree of stiffness and strength.

Solid bridging is easy to install because you use short lengths of lumber the same size as the floor joists. A staggered pattern allows you to end-nail each piece.

To install metal bridging, you mount the nailing flange on the edge of the joist. You can't use these on existing floors without bending down the top flanges.

1. To install a half sheet and stagger joints to miss the seams in the existing floor, snap a chalk line as a guide, and cut one full 4x8 sheet in half using a circular saw.

2. Set a half sheet next to a full sheet to stagger the seams. Leave at least a ¼-in. gap between the edges of the sheets and the walls. This allows the plywood to expand and contract as needed.

3. Drive screws long enough to reach through the old and new floors. Snap a line so you drive them into supporting joists.

TILE TIP: Remember to buy plywood (or another underlayment) with a smooth enough surface—a minimum of voids—to provide full support for the tile.

flexing between individual boards can crack tile or grout joints. Such underlayment can also be used to provide a smooth, level surface over an uneven subfloor. Both types of underlayment should be at least ½ inch thick, no matter what the thickness of the subflooring.

If you plan to install a new subfloor directly over the joists, use two layers, one of at least ⅝-inch exterior plywood (¾-inch is even better), the second of ½-inch exterior plywood or backer board. Check local building codes for guidance.

With plywood, allow a ⅛-inch gap between each sheet and about ¼ inch where sheets meet adjoining walls to allow for expansion and contraction. Attach the plywood to the existing subflooring with construction adhesive and 6d ring-shank nails or 1¼-inch galvanized, all-purpose (drywall-type) screws. If you are using backer board, con-

sult the manufacturer's literature for recommended installation methods. Generally, the boards are embedded in thinset. Drive nails or screws around the panel perimeter about ½ inch in from the edge and 6 inches on center. Then drive fasteners across the face of the panel in rows about 16 inches on center, spacing them 8 to 12 inches apart.

Make sure the heads are set below the surface to avoid stress points that can crack tiles. Joints between backer board panels are typically filled with tile-setting adhesive and taped with fiberglass mesh tape. Fill the joints between plywood panels with floor-patch compound, wood putty, or tile-setting adhesive. After installing the underlayment, sand any rough or splintery surfaces, and make sure the surface is clean and free of debris before installing the tile.

Tiling Over Concrete

In theory, there is no better subfloor for tile than a concrete slab. It has no flex at all, unlike a wood-framed floor, and provides the kind of stable base needed to keep grout seams from cracking. But on some slabs, you may need to do some repair work to create a smooth and level surface.

If there is a fault in the floor, for example, you need to patch it. Start by chipping away any loose or ragged edges using a hammer and cold chisel. (You need to wear eye protection because chips can fly up with great force.) Then prepare the fault for patching by brushing out the dust and debris, and dampening it. Another option is to apply a liquid bonding agent that helps cement stick in the patch area. Fill the crack with cement, and smooth out the surface using a trowel. You should be able to get by with only one coat.

For old concrete slabs that are in good shape structurally, remove any dirt or residue using a mild detergent. Avoid using harsh chemical cleaners such as concrete and driveway cleaning solutions. They may leave a residue that interferes with the adhesive bond.

Allow new concrete floors or walls to cure for at least one month before you install the tile. If a form-release agent or acceleration compound was used on the concrete, it could interfere with a good adhesive bond. If water beads up on the surface rather than being absorbed, it's likely that chemicals have been used. If so, you may have to install an underlayment.

Checking for Moisture

1. To conduct the dampness test, start by cleaning and drying a small section of the floor. Cover it with aluminum foil, and tape down the edges.

2. Wait a day before removing the patch. If the area underneath is dry, water is not seeping up through the floor; the dampness is from condensation.

3. If the concrete under the patch is wet, the dampness must have risen through the floor because the foil stopped condensation from forming.

TILE TIP: Dampness on a concrete floor could be just condensation, or it could be due to water rising from the ground, a condition that could disrupt tile adhesion. This simple test will show where the dampness comes from.

1. Use a cold chisel and a masonry hammer to chip away rough edges of the crack. Deepen shallow areas so that the patch material gets a good hold.

2. Brush out dust and debris, which can decrease adhesion. You may want to dampen the crack or add a bonding agent before troweling in cement.

3. Use a trowel to fill the crack. Cement will do, although one variety, called hydraulic cement, swells slightly as it sets to make a tight bond.

4. Fill minor depressions in a concrete slab with flash-patch material. Spread it using a trowel the way you would spread drywall compound on a wall.

5. Smooth out the patch area using a large trowel that can ride on the finished floor. You can feather flash-patch compound to a fine edge.

TILE TIP: To get the best bond with a patching material, use the chisel to slightly undercut the top edges of the crack to give the patch something to grab.

Establishing Working Lines

Once the pattern has been established, the tile selected, and a suitable surface upon which to lay the tile has been provided, the working lines used to guide the tile installation can be snapped.

Snapping Initial Lines

If the room is relatively square, snap a chalk line along the length of the area down the center of the room. Then, snap a second chalk line across the width of the room so that each chalk line crosses in the approximate center of the room. Check the cross with a framing square to make sure the intersection forms an exact 90-degree angle. These will be your working lines, or layout lines, used to position the tiles.

Starting at the intersection, either dry-lay a row of tiles along each working line, or use a layout stick to determine the location and size of cut tiles. Be sure to include the width of grout joints when setting down the tiles. If a row of partial tiles along one wall is less than $\frac{1}{2}$ tile in width, reposition the tiles so that the cut row is $\frac{1}{2}$ tile or wider. If the layout results in a very narrow row of cut tiles, the grout joints can be made a bit wider to eliminate that row. Otherwise, the layout lines will have to be repositioned. Similarly, if the last tile against the wall is almost the width of a full tile, all the grout joints can be made a bit narrower to fit a full row of tiles in that space. Using this layout method, start laying out the tile from the center of the room, filling in one quadrant at a time.

Lines for Out-of-Square Rooms.

If the room is out-of-square, tiles must be aligned square to at least one wall. To do this, establish a set of square working lines and begin laying out the tiles from one corner of the room. Typically, the lines will be projected from the "most square" corner of the room.

To determine which corner is most square, place a tile tightly against the walls in each corner of the room. Project chalk lines from the outside corner of each tile in both directions; then check the intersections of the chalk lines at each corner for square. Choose the one that is closest to 90 degrees. From this corner, measure out the width of two grout joints and snap a second pair of chalk lines. These will be the working lines. If they are not perfectly square, select the longest wall, or the wall that will be most visible in the room. Then adjust the working line along the adjacent wall until the two working lines form an exact right angle. With the above method, the tiles are laid out from the square corner along the working lines which, if the two walls are square, will result in whole tiles along the two adjacent walls and cut tiles on the walls opposite them.

As with the center-cross layout lines discussed, dry-lay the tiles along the two working lines to determine the size of the cut tiles on the opposite walls. If cut pieces will be less than $\frac{1}{2}$ tile wide and will detract from the installation, adjust the width of the grout joints or reposition the working lines to compensate. Bear in mind that repositioning either of the working lines will cause partial tiles on the wall next to the line that has been moved.

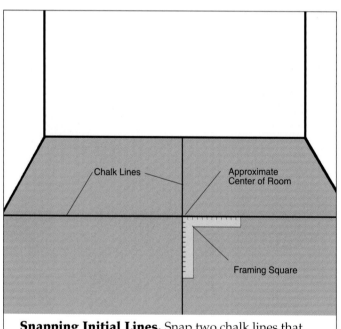

Snapping Initial Lines. Snap two chalk lines that intersect each other at a 90-deg. angle at the approximate center of the room. Check intersection with a framing square.

Lines for Out-of-Square Rooms. For wavy or out-of-square walls, place tiles in each corner of room and snap lines between them. Measure in grout joints to establish working lines. Start tiling from square corner.

Lines for L-Shaped Rooms. Divide the room into two squares or rectangles, and snap layout lines as shown. Adjust the lines so that all intersections are at 90 degrees. Adjust lines as necessary so that cut tiles around the room perimeter will be larger than one-half tile.

Lines for Adjoining Rooms. When extending the tile into an adjoining room, make sure the grout joints line up between the two rooms. If the entrance is wide, try to center the tiles so that any cut tiles at each side are of the same width.

Lines for Large Tiles. Large, irregular-size quarry tiles and pavers generally require additional working lines to ensure that the grout joints align properly and are of approximately the same width. Typically, extra chalk lines are added to form a grid. Each square in the grid can contain four, six, or nine tiles; the lines represent the middle of the grout joints between the tiles. When setting the tile, fill in one block at a time, adjusting the tiles until all of the grout joints are evenly spaced. It is best to dry-lay the tiles in each grid to get the spacing right.

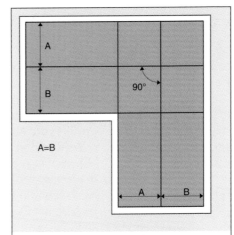

Lines for L-Shaped Rooms. Working lines for an L-shaped room bisect both "legs" of the L. As with a square room, adjust the lines to avoid narrow cuts along walls, and start laying tiles at the intersection of the two lines, filling in one section at a time.

Lines for Diagonal Layouts. When laying tiles diagonally, a second set of working lines will be required. From the intersection of the original working lines, measure out an equal distance along any three of the lines, and drive a nail at these points (A, B, and C, on the drawing). Hook the end of a tape measure to one of the nails and hold a pencil against the tape measure at a distance equal to that between the nails and centerpoint. Use the tape measure and pencil as a compass to scribe two sets of arcs on the floor.

Snap two diagonal chalk lines; one between the center intersection and point D on the drawing below, and one between the center intersection and point E. Extend these lines in each direction to the four walls. Erase or cross out the original working lines and lay the tile to the diagonal ones. Use your layout stick or rows of actual tiles to determine the size of cut tiles at the walls. Adjust the working lines, if necessary, to achieve the best pattern of partial tiles at all four walls. When setting the tiles, fill in one quadrant at a time, using the sequence shown below. In a diagonal layout, the cut tiles will always end up against the walls. Ideally, these will be full diagonal half tiles.

Lines for Adjoining Rooms. Grout joints should line up. If tiles are large, line A may be adjusted so that tiles are centered symmetrically across the opening.

Lines for Large Tiles. Large, irregularly shaped quarry tiles or pavers with wide grout joints are easier to lay out if secondary working lines are provided.

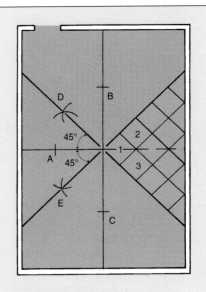

Lines for Diagonal Layouts. A second set of working lines will be needed for a diagonal layout. (See above text.) Lay tiles as shown above.

Installing Floor Tiles

To keep the first rows straight, snap chalk lines along the floor. Work adhesive up to your guidelines using a notched trowel, but don't apply more adhesive than you can cover with tile before the adhesive skins over or sets up. The amount of workable area depends both on the working time of the adhesive and on the speed at which you lay the tiles. Start with a small area, and work up to larger areas as your speed increases.

When you spread the adhesive, use the method and notch size recommended by the tile dealer. Be careful not to cover the working lines with adhesive. For extra-thick tile or tile that has a deep-ridged back pattern, butter the back side with adhesive as well as the floor.

After spreading the adhesive, press a tile into place and twist it slightly—to bed it firmly. You can also use a bedding block to ensure that tiles in a field are flat and firmly embedded. Slide the block (a length of 2×4 wrapped in a carpet scrap) across the tiled surface while tapping it lightly with a hammer or rubber mallet.

Also check tiles frequently with a layout stick to make sure they maintain alignment. You can make small corrections by wiggling the tiles until they are true. If a tile sinks below the surface of surrounding tiles, remove it, add more adhesive, and reset it.

Job Site Safety

Tiling is certainly not the most dangerous kind of construction work. But there are several operations where you need to take sensible precautions and protect yourself.

Ventilation. When working with an organic adhesive or other volatile or toxic material, you need to provide ventilation according to the manufacturer's recommendations. Bear this in mind when you are using cleaning materials, too. Check product labels for cautions. You may also need to wear a respirator and safety gloves.

Cutting. Snap cutters are safe tools to use because handle positions are removed from the cutting and splitting action. Nippers are also safe if you use them correctly and take only very small bites. You need to take more care using a wet saw. Although wet-saw blades generally don't have cutting teeth, the coated abrasive edge spins at high speed. The sensible approach is to keep your hands at the sides of the feed table; then be sure that the tile is firmly seated, and feed the tile into the blade gradually.

Laying Out Floors

Laser levels emit a light beam that shows clearly on almost any surface. The tools are used mainly to establish level points. But they also are handy in tile work, where they can project layout lines.

Battery-powered laser levels project a beam of light. You can use one to establish level points or to display working guidelines on floors and walls

With a laser layout line projected across the floor, you don't have to hold back adhesive to keep from covering the line the way you must with chalk lines.

1. You can plan the layout based only on measurements, but it's wise to set out a few rows on your snapped lines and see how the field fits the room. This will also help you determine the size of cut tiles along the borders.

2. Use a notched trowel to spread the tile adhesive up to your guidelines. Match the notch depth to the adhesive and tile type.

3. Set the tiles into the ribbed adhesive bed. You need only moderate pressure to embed them and create a secure bond.

4. Set spacers to maintain the grid layout. Some spacers may remain under grout; others must be removed. (Check with the manufacturer.) Using spacers ensures consistent grout lines.

5. Use your layout stick every few rows or so to check the tile alignment. You can also make sure the grid is square by measuring from the walls.

TILE TIP: Chalk lines can mark the center of the room, and also set up working guidelines if you snap them along grout seams.

1. To mark border tiles, set a full tile on top of the tile at the edge of the field, and another tile on it to find and mark the margin to the wall.

2. Use a snap cutter to score the surface of the tile along your mark. You need to draw the scoring arm toward you with firm pressure.

3. On most tiles, you need to draw the scoring wheel across the surface firmly but only once to slice through the glaze and get a clean snap.

4. To break the tile cleanly, most snap cutters have a handle connected to a pressure plate that pushes down evenly on both sides of the score line.

5. Use a notched trowel to spread adhesive along the edge of the tile field. Then set the partial tile in place using spacers if need be.

6. On partial tiles that meet an obstruction along the edge of the room, you can use a scoring tool to crack the glaze before cutting with a nipper.

7. Start nipping very small pieces of the cutout section, working gradually up to your cut line. You may want to file cut edges in exposed installations.

8. Fit the trimmed partial tile into place. Remember to leave enough space for grout or caulk.

TILE TIP: On edge cuts you can often save time with the tile nipper (and some broken tiles) by first scoring and cutting off a waste section with a snap cutter.

Cutting Partial Tiles

If you start with full tiles in a corner, you can get into trouble when the field reaches the opposite walls. To avoid cutting uneven pieces, you should lay the main field in the center of the room so that you can use partial tiles of the same size around the edges. This approach also makes the job go faster.

In situations where the layout won't allow equal sizes of partial tiles, the best plan is to use full tiles in the most visible portion of the room, and save the small or irregular pieces for a less important or partially concealed border—for example, the wall normally concealed behind an open door.

When all of the full tiles in the main field are down, cut and place all the partial tiles around the room perimeter. If you plan to use cove or trim tiles, you have to allow for the thickness (and a grout joint) against the wall. If the field tiles run to the wall, leave a slight gap between the tiles and wall for expansion.

Offset Measuring. To cut partial field and border tiles, place a loose tile directly on top of the full-size tile next to the space to be filled. Place another loose tile on top of that one, and move it against the wall. Use the back edge of that top tile as a guide, and draw a line on the surface of the loose tile below. That's the one you cut. This offset method of measuring is also handy if you need to trim L-shaped tiles at corners.

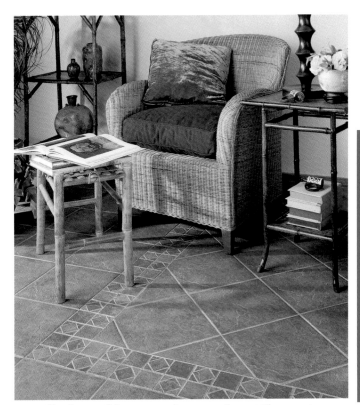

A well-planned layout and accurately cut tiles create an appealing living space.

Thresholds

Thresholds (sometimes called saddles) can be wood, metal, or marble strips that bridge gaps between different types of floors. They can also make a transition between floors that are almost but not quite level with each other—for example, where a tiled bath floor is slightly higher than the wood floor in a hallway. You attach the threshold to the underlayment and tile up to it. Most wood and metal saddles are attached with nails or screws. (You can conceal the screw heads in wooden saddles with putty or plugs.) Marble saddles, which are typically used at bathroom doors, are set in a bed of adhesive. Whatever type you use, plan for thresholds during the layout stage.

Wooden Threshold

Caulk

Tile on Backer Board   Wooden Threshold   Oak Flooring   Subfloor

Metal Threshold

Caulk

Tile on Backer Board   Metal Threshold   Carpet   Subfloor

Marble Threshold

Tile

Backer Board

Marble Threshold   Parquet Flooring   Subfloor

Applying the Grout

Before you grout the tile joints, the adhesive has to cure. That could take 24 to 48 hours. Check the manufacturer's recommendations to be sure. Then take the time to clean any dirt or debris from the joints, and remove spacers, if necessary.

If you are using tile that is easily stained, you can protect the surface with a removable sealer. Make sure the sealer has cured fully before applying the grout. Generally, ceramic tiles do not become stained from grout—or almost anything else. It's normally the grout itself that becomes stained.

Mix the grout according to manufacturer's instructions. Plan on mixing enough to fill all the seams. Even over a large area, grout goes down quickly. Most people have success using a rubber float to spread grout, but you can also try a squeegee. Plunk down a trowel full of the material, and start working it into the joints by sweeping your float at a diagonal to the field pattern. You need to sweep the float back and forth, pushing the pile of grout, making several passes over the same area to compact the grout into the joints.

Do not use grout to fill the joint between the last row of floor tiles and the wall. Instead, use flexible silicone caulk to allow for expansion and contraction between the different materials.

As soon as the grout becomes firm, use a wet sponge to wipe off excess grout from the tile surface. You might use a squeegee to clear any streaks of grout material; then start with the sponge. On most jobs it takes several passes (rinsing the sponge frequently and changing the water, too) before the final grout haze is cleaned up.

Tooling and Sealing Joints

You may be able to leave the grout joints flush, or nearly flush, just by working the seams with your trowel. Another option is to tool, or strike, the joints to create slightly recessed seams. (You can also do this before cleaning the excess.) Many common objects can do the job, including a toothbrush handle, small spoon, or a shaped stick.

Clean off the tiles again, and smooth the joints using a damp sponge. This will leave yet another haze that you can polish away with a clean, damp cloth. In most cases, the grout will take several days to cure completely. You may need to wait longer before applying a sealer; check the grout label directions.

In wet areas (mainly bathrooms) you can retard surface mold and protect grout seams by adding a sealer, such as liquid silicone. Start in the corner farthest away from the door, and apply a thin, even coat of sealer on the grout only. Some sealers come with a built-in applicator, or you can use an artist's brush.

1. On most jobs, the best approach is to mix only the grout you need. You can buy color-matched grout or add powdered colorant to the mix.

2. Use a float (or a squeegee) to push the grout into the seams. Make sweeping strokes at a diagonal to the grid pattern of the tile field. This will help you work the grout into all of the joints.

3. When the grout sets up (you may want to strike off the seams first), start to clean up the remaining surface glaze using a clean, damp sponge.

4. Even after several passes with a sponge, you may need to remove a final haze by polishing the tile surface using a clean, damp cloth.

5. In wet areas such as kitchens and baths, consider one more step: sealing the grout seams (generally with a liquid silicone) to reduce maintenance.

TILE TIP: To wipe off the grout haze, use several large sponges, rinsing in clean water after every few passes. Without regular rinsing, you'll just respread the haze. Change the water frequently.

3 Tiling Floors

tiling walls

MORE THAN ANY OTHER SURFACE, perhaps, walls provide an opportunity to combine decoration and durability. In fact, you may find more choices in wall tiles than in any other kind.

At the other end of the spectrum, a wall can serve as a blank canvas for unique, hand-painted tile murals or bold designs of contrasting colors and shapes. Most tile is available with edging components to trim partial installations.

Because tiles resist heat, water, and a variety of stains, they are well suited to kitchen and bathroom walls where easy maintenance is a prime concern. In kitchens, of course, tiles often bridge the gap between countertops and upper cabinets. You also find tile used on walls behind sinks and stoves.

In bathrooms, tile is often used to line shower stalls and tub surrounds. But you can give a bathroom a more open, unified feeling by extending the tile to adjacent walls. Behind a vanity, you can extend a tile backsplash up the wall to frame a mirror. And wall tiles with trim strips can frame windows, doors, and other architectural features in any room of the house.

Design and Layout

The same basic design considerations that apply to floors—color, size, shape, texture, and pattern—also apply to walls. However, when planning your layout, bear in mind that most wall applications incorporate a design that uses tiles of contrasting colors. This makes estimating the number of tiles a bit more difficult and requires a more precise layout.

Tile work on walls often involves different types and shapes of trim pieces, such as tiles with a bullnose edge. You may also need to use special shapes to handle inside and outside corners. These special shapes can make a tile job look very elegant, but they complicate the layout. You need to account for the grout joints, of course, but also for the odd-size portion of the trim piece that turns an inside or outside corner.

If you plan to tile both the walls and the floor, you have two sets of layouts to deal with. Each one may require an adjustment to make a balanced installation, but you need to concentrate on the area along the floor where the two systems meet. You should align grout seams there, if at all possible.

One approach is to start these projects by installing the row of cove or other finishing tiles at the floor level. Coves make a very low-maintenance detail (a great help in kitchens and baths) because the rounded cove base eliminates hard-edged, dirt-trapping corners.

Because this row makes the transition between floor and wall, it's important to have full tiles on both sides if possible. That means you can't adjust the main tile field of the floor on one side, or the wall on the other, which could

leave small, partial tiles at the opposite wall or the ceiling. The best bet is to lay out tiles with spacers for grout joints (or make an accurate layout stick) and see where the field tiles will fall.

Once you have positioned the cove tiles, you can work your way up the wall. Save the floor for last so that you don't damage or blemish the new tile with adhesive or grout as you work on the wall.

Patterns and Unique Designs

Many tile manufacturers now make integrated tile systems. For example, in addition to field tiles, they offer rectangular pieces for borders, half-round accent strips, caps, and several other shapes all designed to work in the same basic grid. With these systems it is relatively easy to plan out a repeating wall scheme, and the grout seams will align.

If you are creating your own design, the amount of detail you can include is determined in part by three elements: the size of the wall, the size of the design, and the size of the tiles. Bear in mind that geometric patterns are the easiest to create and install because the basic building blocks are geometric units. It's more difficult to create and install a free-flowing pattern. For example, if you want to create a curved design along a set of stairs, you will have to make many precise cuts.

Cutting Tiles

A good layout plan will help determine in advance where you need cut tiles. The trick is arranging the main field so that you do not end up with a narrow row in a conspicuous place.

Cut tiles should be more than half a tile wide. Ideally, they should be equal widths at opposite sides of a room to provide symmetry. Sometimes you can adjust the edge sizes by adjusting the width of all the grout joints.

Also be aware of where cut tiles may be needed around doorways, windows, cabinets, and countertops, and whether it would look better to plan the layout so that partial tiles are moved away from these focal points. For example, cut tiles on either side of a window or door opening should be the same width for the opening to appear centered. In the same way, if you are tiling around a fireplace, the wall installation will probably look best if you use full tiles on the sides and save partial tiles or irregular pieces for the corners of the room.

Planning for Materials

To estimate the amount of tiles you need, disregard small obstructions when you're measuring square footage. Subtract only for a large window, built-in sink, or cabinet. It's wise to figure about 5 to 10 percent for waste. If your installation includes different-color tiles, use your drawing to count the actual number of tiles of each color, adding the same percentage for miscuts and breakage. If the layout includes cut tiles, count each partial tile as a full tile.

If you are extending tile to adjoining walls or across a doorway, you will want to align the horizontal grout joints. It's often best to use full tiles where walls join, but you should check how the field tiles will fall when they reach the edges of the project area. If you center full tiles over a doorway, for example, you might end up with cut tiles of two different widths at opposite ends of the wall. You can't very well reshape your rooms to match a tile grid. But if you check several possible layouts, you can generally find one that has full tiles where you notice the pattern

and partial tiles where you don't.

If you're working with mural tiles (or almost any distinct pattern within the main tile field), you may need to account for a large block of tiles. Most murals come in sets of tiles—from as few as four to well over 50—with each tile representing a piece of the picture. Plan these installations by taking the overall dimensions of the mural and adjusting the set of tiles on the wall. You may be able to balance the layout on a wall and avoid small pieces at the corners by using border tiles.

Design Options

No design is bad if it's in your own house and represents the style you like. Colors and patterns are matters of personal taste, after all. But before you undertake a tile project covering most or all of a wall, it pays to experiment.

You can do this on a piece of graph paper, using colored pencils to sketch in your ideas at a realistic scale. And you can rummage through tile supply houses trying different combinations. But also consider design services that are increasingly available to do-it-yourselfers.

If you have a home computer, you may be able to use home-design software to create tile patterns complete with bath fixtures, lights, and a mirror.

Now some home-center chains and design-build contracting firms also offer computer-aided design (CAD) services. They allow you to plan a layout for a specific wall area and try different combinations of tile. The most sophisticated software creates three-dimensional views showing how the finished project might look, although they may dress up the view with stock furniture and other fixtures.

Computer-aided design software programs let you experiment using different tile patterns and colors on your home computer screen.

Using computer design programs, you can create a rough view of an area using stock versions of rugs and other fixtures to build your "before" picture.

Define the area you want to change, the floor in this case, and insert different shapes and patterns that change carpeting into tile.

You can use different sizes, shapes, and colors to create a nearly limitless number of tile patterns and combinations. But even if you stick to one size, there are three basic ways to set them on the wall.

Jack-on-Jack. This is the easiest way to lay wall tiles, stacking one tile directly on top of another.

Running Bond. This is the same kind of pattern used on most brick walls, with the joints of one course centered under full tiles in the next row.

Diagonal Jack-on-Jack. This is the basic system of aligned joints turned sideways 45 degrees, which makes square tiles look diamond-shaped. The drawback is that every tile in the rows at the floor and ceiling have to be trimmed.

Jack-on-jack layouts have tiles stacked directly on top of each other in columns. With this system, all the grout joints between tiles are aligned.

Running bond layouts have the joints in one course offset to fall over the center of tiles below. The offset is accentuated with contrasting colors.

Diagonal jack-on-jack layouts have the basic stacked tile pattern turned sideways on the wall. This gives square tiles a diamond-shaped appearance.

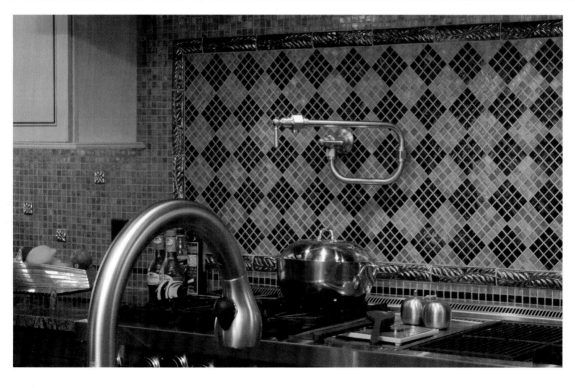

One approach is to plan the main field, and then see where you can add a repeating pattern of accent tiles.

Preparing Walls for Tile

Most interior walls are surfaced with gypsum wallboard. In many older homes, the walls are plastered. Both materials generally make a good backing for ceramic tile if the surface is sound, flat, and smooth. You also can tile over sound wood or masonry walls. It's not a good idea to tile over wallpaper, fabric, or any other surface that is not strong enough by itself to support tile.

In new construction, of course, a taped and finished drywall surface will make an ideal base for tile. But in existing rooms you may have to make some repairs and improvements to be sure that the tile job will last. There are two basic options: bury surface problems under a new layer of drywall, or fix the existing wall.

In addition to the surface repairs, you may want to make some changes that are more than skin deep, such as relocating an electrical outlet or moving an in-wall air conditioner. If there are problems with the wall framing, you should strip off the old surface, fix the problems, and install new drywall. Remember that tile needs exceptionally firm support to keep grout joints from cracking. If there is movement in the wall—for instance, due to a water leak—the tile job isn't likely to last.

Wall Strength

Generally, a wall is considered too weak for tile if you can flex the surface by pressing the heel of your hand against a panel midway between two studs. Adding another layer of drywall should do the trick, but even ½ inch of extra

---

Extending an Electrical Box

1. First, be sure that power is off at the box in question, and confirm this with a tester. Then release the holding screws on the outlet or switch.

2. Use the screws to fasten a code-approved box extension, which will bring the outlet or switch flush with the new tile wall.

3. Make a cutout in the backer board to accommodate the box extension, and set the box extension, allowing for the thickness of the tile.

TILE TIP: Extending an electrical box accommodates any new backing material and the new tile you will install on the wall. If you don't extend the box, the receptacle or the switch will be set back from the surface of the wall, which may be a code violation.

Wall tiles in wet areas around baths and sinks should be supported by panels of cement-based backer board.

wall thickness can pose problems around window and door trim.

You can refasten loose panels with drywall screws spaced 8 to 10 inches apart along all framing members. You can locate studs and other framing behind the wall with an inexpensive magnetic stud finder.

If the panels are too thin or weak to support the tile, a second layer of ½-inch wallboard or cement backer board over the existing panels will provide extra rigidity. When covering existing panels with new ones, make sure that the joints between the new panels do not fall directly over those in the existing wall.

If necessary, you can reinforce wall framing with blocking or additional studs. In general, studs should have a maximum spacing of 16 inches on center, and wallboard or other backing materials should be a minimum of ½ inch thick.

Existing Wall Surfaces

On walls covered with paneling or wallpaper, you'll need to strip the old surface. Paneling is easy enough to remove; you just pull the trim and pry off the sheets. Removing wallpaper can be trickier.

You can roll on a liquid wallpaper remover or rent a steamer box to loosen the paper adhesive. These sys-tems generally work better if you first scuff up the paper surface with a scarifying tool. When you scrape away the residue, try not to dig into the drywall surface.

Even if the wallboard or plaster is sound, you should not set tile if the surface paint is loose or peeling. Prepare these surfaces basically the same way you would for re-painting. Start by scraping away any loose paint. Then fill deep gouges using joint compound.

Walls in Wet Areas

If you are tiling a wall that is subject to moisture—for ex-ample, behind a kitchen sink or in a bathroom—you need to install some type of waterproofing membrane, water-re-sistant backing, or both. The most common application is a layer of cement-based backer board attached with cor-rosion-resistant nails or screws.

Depending on the extent of moisture exposure, a wa-terproof membrane also may be required. This is an im-portant step that many do-it-yourselfers make the mistake of omitting. There are several types, including liquid mem-branes and the old standby, 15-pound roofing felt. The most common (and the one recommended for backer board) is 4-mil polyethylene sheets. You may want to check local building codes for recommended waterproof-ing materials.

1. Once you get a piece of trim loose using a hammer and screwdriver, apply gradual pressure with a pry bar to move it away from the wall.

2. To remove large pieces of baseboard trim without damaging the wall, insert a wooden shim behind the board when you pry.

3. On long boards, you may need to use several screwdrivers, chisels, or similar tools as wedges while you work the piece free.

4. To remove stubborn nails, set a bar between the nail points and the wall, and tap on the baseboard to expose the heads so that you can pull them.

5. Label the location of each piece as you remove it. On a room with many corners, this will make it easier to reinstall the trim.

TILE TIP: Trim in an older home can be very brittle and easy to break. If you plan to reinstall it, pry gently, gradually working your way along the boards.

Patching Drywall

The good news is that you don't have to patch every minor dent and scratch, because they will be filled by the tile adhesive. But you should repair holes and fix popped nails, bubbled joint tape, and other problems that could keep the tile from sitting flat on the wall.

Instead of driving loose nails back into drywall, pull them and drive a drywall screw near the old hole. Along joints, check for splits or bubbles in the drywall tape. If you find raised or loose sections, slice the damaged tape from the wall using a utility knife, and replace it with fiberglass mesh tape embedded in the tile adhesive.

There are several ways to repair larger cracks and holes. The most drastic is to cut out a section of the damaged drywall running from one stud to another, although this entails so much cutting that you might as well replace the entire sheet. In most cases, you can add mesh to reinforce a patch or cut out the damaged area and add a patch piece of solid drywall.

Over small holes—for example, where you have some crumbling around holes for plumbing pipes—you can use self-stick fiberglass mesh to bridge the gaps and reinforce a filling layer of joint compound. For doorknob-size holes, you can use a mesh patch kit that comes with an extra reinforcing panel.

One good way to fix large holes is to cut a clean-edged rectangular opening around the damage, and reinforce the edges with short lengths of 1×3 fastened to the inside face of the drywall. The exposed edges of the wood strips can support a solid drywall patch.

Patching Small Holes

1. Bridge small holes and gaps using self-stick fiberglass mesh tape. It keeps patch material from falling through the hole and reinforces the repair.

2. Joint compound will embed in the mesh. You will probably need one coat to fill the hole and another to smooth over the surface.

3. Over larger holes, you can use a self-stick patch kit. Peel off the backing; install the reinforcing panel face down; and finish the mesh surface.

TILE TIP: When you're making a repair, don't try to save sections or edges of drywall that seem weak. Cut back until you reach solid material that will support the new tile.

Preparing and Repairing Plaster

Extensive cracking in a plaster wall often indicates regular seasonal movement in the building, which can disrupt tile. In severe cases, you may need to strip the surface, although a layer of glued-and-screwed cement backer board may work. If the plaster is soft and cracks or crumbles when you poke it with a screwdriver, it should be removed.

Fill small holes or depressions with patching plaster. Clean and moisten the area, and spread the fresh plaster using a wide drywall taping knife. When the patch dries, fill it to the surface, let it dry, and sand it flush.

If the plaster is sound, wash it thoroughly using a general-purpose cleaner to remove dirt or grease. Sand a glossy painted surface to ensure a good adhesive bond.

Repairing Outside Corners

Corners that project into a room (around pass-through openings, for example) often take the most abuse and show the most damage—both in drywall and plaster walls. If the damage is minor, you can usually repair it using drywall joint compound and a wide drywall knife. Use a straightedge to shape the corner edge, or smooth out one side and let it dry before you work on the adjoining surface.

If the damage is extensive, you may need to cut away the corner reinforcement. Although some corners may have only paper-taped edges that are easy to remove, most have metal corner guards secured with nails. Once the guard is damaged, you may have to pull the nails and remove it (or a piece of it) and install new edging.

Patching Plaster

1. Use patching plaster to fill the damaged area in layers. Score the undercoat surface. When dry, moisten before troweling on the finish coat.

2. Use a wide blade to smooth out the finish coat. Let one edge ride on the adjacent wall to keep the patch flush. Sand down any ridges.

3. When the finish coat is dry, prime the patch to keep the dry, unsealed material from drawing moisture from the tile adhesive.

TILE TIP: It's wise to seal large areas of fresh plaster or joint compound so that the dry material does not pull excessive moisture from the tile adhesive and weaken the tile bond.

1. To get at a damaged section of corner guard, you may have to cut through layers of paint and joint compound using a utility knife.

2. Once the guard is exposed, use a hacksaw to cut through the metal above and below the damaged section. Pull the nails, and remove it.

3. Use metal snips to cut a replacement length of guard. Fold as shown so that the cut is even on both sides. Clear away loose drywall paper and compound on the corner before you fasten the piece.

4. Use drywall screws to fasten the replacement guard on the corner. Place the new piece of corner guard carefully, making sure that the raised corner rib aligns with the original guard.

5. Provide a flat surface for the tile by filling in both sides of the raised corner rib using joint compound. Sand off any raised ridges.

TILE TIP: If the corner guard has a dent in it but is still secure, try filling the area using joint compound. Always replace a loose guard.

4 Tiling Walls

Installing New Drywall

Here are a few of the key steps involved in drywall, and some tips on making the job solid enough to support tile securely.

- **Installation Efficiency.** Most do-it-yourselfers use 4 × 8 sheets standing on end. It's a nice match for standard 8-foot ceiling height, but you can also install sheets horizontally, creating one tape seam down the middle of the wall.

- **Cutting Holes.** The tool of choice for pros is a pint-sized router with a long straight bit. It can plunge through drywall and closely follow the irregular outline of an electrical box. Most DIY-ers have an easier time controlling a straight-handled utility saw made to cut drywall. Its sharp tip allows you to poke through drywall and start a cut. You can also use a utility knife, but it's difficult (and more dangerous) to use a knife to carve through interior cuts, where a saw offers more control.

- **Long Cuts.** Even many pros use a 4-foot-long metal T-square to guide a utility knife in a full-width cut through a sheet. Along the 8-foot length of a panel you can snap a chalk guideline. You don't need to press hard on the knife to make the scoring cut. It's more important to slice a straight line than to dig deeply, even if you have to go over your cut again. Then you can snap the panel along the score line, and trim through the remaining paper.

- **Lifters.** Whether you install sheets vertically or horizontally, the edge resting on the floor has to be raised a bit before you nail. In many houses, the bottom edge will be covered by baseboard trim, while the top edge will form a visible taped and finished joint. Make this job easier by using a panel lifter—a wedge-shaped tool that seesaws over a built-in wheel. Kick the lifter under the edge of the sheet, and step down on one end; the other end lifts the panel into position quite easily, leaving your hands free.

- **Nails and Screws.** Do-it-yourselfers normally use nails and a hammer to hang gypsum drywall. Most pros favor screws and a power screwdriver because it's faster and easier, and the screwheads leave small dimples that are easy to finish. You may want to use a nail or two to hold the sheet in place at first. Then you can step back, load up the drill, and fasten the rest of the sheet using screws.

- **Taping.** You should be able to get by with only one coat of compound on field fasteners and taped seams. Don't leave any large ridges that could prevent tiles from seating against the wall.

Installing Drywall

1. It's easy enough to measure the overall width you need. But you have to measure very carefully to locate an outlet or switch in the panel section.

2. Locate the sides of the box and measure up from the bottom of the sheet to find its height. Always double-check measurements before cutting.

3. Use the sharp tip of a utility saw to poke through the panel at the corners of the box. Then you can cut along the marks with the saw teeth.

4. To trim the drywall panel to overall size, mark or snap a cutting guideline and score along the mark using a sharp utility knife.

5. Slide the panel waste section beyond its supports, and snap down to crack the gypsum in a straight line. Then slice through the backing paper.

6. Use a panel lifter to raise the drywall into place. Your weight supplies the lifting power, leaving your hands free to position and fasten the sheet.

7. Use a variable-speed drill to drive wide-threaded wallboard screws. They provide more holding power and are less likely to pop out than nails.

8. To prepare new drywall for tile, a one- or two-coat taping job should do. Fill feathered panel edges so that the tile will be evenly supported.

TILE TIP: Use ⅜-in. panels to resurface walls because they are stiffer than ¼-in. sheets.

Installing Wall Tile

Installing wall tile follows the same general procedures as installing floor tile. But you lay wall tiles from the lowest point up so that the tiles and spacers can support the next course. Most adhesives used for wall tile are formulated to hold the tiles in place while still wet. These include thinset latex-portland cement and organic mastic adhesives.

Establishing Working Lines

On simple wall installations, you can establish a vertical working line near the base of the wall and a horizontal line at or near the center point of the wall. Then you start laying tiles at the intersection of the two lines.

Additional layout lines are helpful if the wall is large or contains openings, counters, cabinets, or other built-in fixtures. It is also a good idea to add lines that locate trim and border tiles. Carefully measured guidelines help you position field tiles in a balanced layout and keep joints aligned as the job progresses.

In most cases, you establish a vertical working line at or near the center of the wall. If the wall has a large window or other opening, you may want to adjust the vertical line so that the opening is centered and tiles on both sides of the opening are the same width.

To establish the vertical line, measure the width of the tiled area, and mark the center point. Use your layout stick (or a row of spaced tiles on the floor) to mark off tile and grout joints on either side of this point.

Planning the Layout

If the last tile at each end is going to be more than half a tile wide, you can use the center point to establish the vertical guideline. If the end tiles are going to be less than half a tile wide, move the vertical guideline a distance of half a tile to the right or left of the centerline. This will result in wider partial tiles at each end.

You also need to establish a level horizontal baseline to ensure that the first row—and all rows above it—will be level. If the wall includes a countertop, vanity, or tub and you are tiling the wall from floor level, you may have to adjust the baseline at the floor.

Usually, it looks best to have full tiles above these features even if it means having a row of cut tiles at floor level. If you are tiling only partway up the wall, establish another horizontal guide to indicate the limit line.

A Tiling Sequence

There are two basic ways to lay field tile on a wall. You can build up the tiles from the center of the wall in a pyramid shape, or lay the length of the bottom row and work from one corner. Remember that most layouts look best with the full field tiles centered and equal partial tiles at the edges.

If you use trim tiles at floor level, you typically set all of them first and then fill in above them with field tiles. Trim pieces for inside and outside corners are installed just ahead of the whole field tiles, and cut pieces are filled in as needed.

In all cases, you will be building the tile up from the bottom, including grout joint spacers. Each new course is supported by the course beneath it.

1. Starting in the center of the tile area, use your layout stick to transfer a set of carefully measured tile and grout marks to the wall surface. (See "Making a Layout Stick," on page 31.)

2. At the edges of the layout area, use a full tile to determine what the margin will be on the cut-tile edges. About half a tile is an ideal margin.

3. Once the vertical layout is settled, use a level to establish a horizontal line. To extend level marks on a large wall, set the level on a straight 2x4.

4. To leave a clear chalk residue as you snap a line, temporarily pin the line with your finger at midspan, and snap one side and then the other.

5. Use your level to establish a vertical guideline. It's convenient to snap chalk lines on a layout stick tick mark, so you can follow it exactly with tiles.

6. Complete your guides with another snapped chalk line. You may want other guides to indicate rows of trim and areas around obstructions.

7. Mark the location of built-in nailers for grab bars or other wall fittings on the floor. Marks on the wall will be obscured by adhesive and then tile. For finished flooring, write the dimensions on tape that you will remove later.

TILE TIP: To preserve guidelines and save time spreading adhesive, mask key lines with tape. You can trowel over the tape and remove it later to reveal a crisp edge of adhesive.

1

1. Establish a level baseline for the field tiles. Measure up from the floor's high point, allowing for full tiles with grout joints.

2. One approach is to support the field tiles and prevent sagging using pairs of nails. You install the bottom row after the field tiles have set.

3. Prepare to set the field tiles above the nails by spreading adhesive recommended by the tile manufacturer using a notched trowel.

4. Set the field tiles into the adhesive bed using light pressure. Work in a limited area up to a guideline before spreading more adhesive.

5. Use spacers in grout seams to maintain alignment and to

2

3

5

6

7

help transfer weight down to the first row, which is supported by the nails.

6. When the main field is secure, you can pull the nails and set the bottom row. Tape prevents sagging so that the floor-level seam won't close up.

7. When all the tiles are fixed in place, spread the grout using a float. Use sweeping strokes on diagonals to the tile grid system to fill the seams.

8. Grout leaves a haze even if you finish with a squeegee to remove residue. You need several passes using a clean, damp sponge to clear it away.

TILE TIP: To avoid stress cracks, use caulk instead of grout on the floor-level seam.

Cutting Tiles

Use a snap tile cutter to make straight cuts, and a pair of nippers, if necessary, to notch around irregular shapes. If the tiles you're using have ridges on the back, it may help to cut in the same direction that the ridges run. If you want to make a clean hole in the tile to fit around a pipe or other wall fitting, use a carbide-tipped hole saw.

Applying Adhesive

Apply just enough adhesive for you to cover with tile before it skins over or sets up. That area depends on how fast you work, of course, and on the open time of the adhesive. On large walls, start with small sections of about 4 × 4 feet, and spread more adhesive once you get a sense of the working time.

Spread the adhesive using the manufacturer-recommended method and notched-trowel size. Some adhesives are best spread at an angle to the tile, while others are best spread in overlapping arcs. Be careful not to cover your working lines with adhesive. Keep the appropriate solvent on hand to clean your trowel and wipe up spills as you work.

Laying the Tile

After spreading the adhesive, press each tile into place with a slight twisting motion to embed it. Do not slide tiles against each other, or you will end up with excess adhesive in the joints. If adhesive does bulk up, clean it out before it hardens.

As you lay the tiles, frequently check their alignment with a level, and make sure you maintain uniform grout spacing. Also check the wall surface with a straightedge periodically to make sure that all the tiles are seated the same way. If you find one that's raised, use more pressure to set it before the adhesive sets up. If you use too much pressure on a tile and embed it below the others, pry it out, butter the back with adhesive, and reset it flush.

When the installation requires a row of cut tiles, do not presume that they will all be the same size. You may have to check each one and adjust its size where the squared-up tile field meets a ceiling that isn't level with the floor or an adjacent wall that isn't plumb with the field.

Finishing

Use a float to spread grout into the joints. Work the float with diagonal sweeps to force the material thoroughly into the seams. Where the tile meets the floor, use a flexible caulk to fill the joint and avoid cracking at this intersection of different materials.

tiling countertops

A CERAMIC OR STONE TILE COUNTER should outlast hardwood or plastic laminate because it's tougher and won't scorch. Expensive, poured-in-place concrete is probably sturdier than tile, and it's joint-free, too. But it can't offer the variations in color and pattern you get with ceramic or stone tile. Another option is to place ceramic or stone tile insets into another counter material, such as solid surfacing.

Planning the Layout

You can buy tile to meet the needs of a specific counter, or modify a new counter (or a replacement over existing cabinets) to fit your new tile. Modifying the counter is a good approach because it's easy to trim an extra inch or so off a sheet of plywood and backer board. And by deciding on your layout ahead of time, you may be able to create a countertop of full field tile and edging pieces.

To see how different edging styles will work, the best approach in the confined area of a countertop is to do a dry layout, using spacers to allow for grout seams. Here are some of the design issues to consider.

- **Counter Edging.** There are several ways to trim the counter edge with tile. The most common is to install V-cap matched to the field tiles. It creates a neat border with no grout joint at the outer edge, and covers the backer board and plywood. You also can use bullnose tiles along the edge or even a strip of wood.
- **Backsplashes.** Some tile backsplashes extend up to the bottom of the wall cabinets. Take its thickness into account when planning the countertop field, and don't forget to include the tiles themselves on drywall, or tiles plus a backer board in wet areas. You also can use tiles with a cove base to make an easy-cleaning seam.

Countertop Options

Front Edge Options

Wood Trim
Backer Board · Caulk · Rounded Edge · Screw and Adhesive · Wood Plug

Bullnose Tile
Adhesive · Grout · Thinset · Trim Tile · Cabinet Face

V-Cap Tile
Grout · Molded Rim · Thinset · Rounded Edge

Backsplash Options

Capped Top
Drywall · Cap · Grout · Thinset · Backer Board · Thinset Tile Bed · Tile · Caulk

Coved Base
Trim Tile · Grout · Thinset · Drywall · Cove · Caulk

Bullnose Return
Rounded Edge · Thinset · Drywall · Caulk

Preparing Countertops

Whether you strip the surface material off an old counter or install a new one, the surface has to be level, smooth, and rigid enough to resist movement that could crack grout joints. The best approach is to install a layer of plywood and a layer of cement backer board. The plywood is typically ¾-inch exterior grade with one finished side.

Strengthening Cabinets

Before you install the counter, build in extra strength to resist even slight shifting. On the cabinets, you may need to add shims, construction adhesive, and some screws to make sure that separate components are tied together and locked into the wall studs. On new corner units, such as lazy Susans, you may need to add nailers along the wall. The supporting frame also has to be level.

Strengthening Counters

On a new counter, rip the leftover plywood into long strips about 3 inches wide to reinforce the back of the main panel. Install the strips with glue and screws along the perimeter, and add cross strips where the counter makes contact with the cabinet partitions.

Construction adhesive at all contact points helps the counter stick to the cabinets. But you also have to squeeze into the confined spaces and drive screws up through cabinet braces into the bottom of the plywood counter. Cabinets generally have either hardware fittings or triangular pieces of wood at the corners for attachment.

Building Countertops

Counter Options

On counters that won't get wet, you can affix tile directly to the plywood. Use either an epoxy adhesive (generally reserved for installations needing resistance to chemicals and solvents) or the type most homeowners and pros use: organic adhesive, generally called thinset.

But thinset applications that are commonly used on floors and walls are not recommended for kitchen and bathroom counters. Where surfaces get wet, there are two other types of installations. With the old-fashioned approach, generally called thickset, you embed tile in a ¾- to 1-inch-thick bed of metal-reinforced cement mortar leveled over a membrane such as roofing felt. It's a solid system but time-consuming and challenging to float a smooth and level mortar bed.

The more modern wet-area installation starts with a moisture-resistant membrane stapled to the plywood—either 15-pound roofing felt or 4-mil polyethylene, although there are also liquid membranes. The poly works well because it not only protects the plywood base of your counter, if you cut it long and drape sheets over the cabinet fronts, it protects them during part of the construction process. Trim the membrane before you tile the counter edge.

Next comes a layer of cement-based backer board set in a bed of thinset combed out in a ribbed pattern using a notched trowel. The adhesive manufacturer determines the notch size needed. You can cut the heavy panels to size with a diamond blade, but it's easier to score and snap them. Use fiberglass mesh tape on the seams.

1. Rip narrow strips off excess plywood to reinforce the counter. Use a table saw or a circular saw with a straightedge guide.

2. Reinforce the plywood counter by attaching the strips along the perimeter with glue and screws. Also install crosspieces over cabinet supports.

3. Use construction adhesive on the cabinet frames to help secure the countertop. Also, cover the partition frames between components.

4. Drive holding screws up through corner braces inside the cabinets. Use screws that drive into (but not through) the layers of plywood.

5. Install a moisture-resistant membrane over the plywood counter. You can use 15-lb. felt paper or 4-mil polyethylene sheeting.

6. Spread an embedding layer of thinset, and install a layer of cement backer board. Leave about a ⅛-in. gap between the panels.

7. Use fiberglass mesh tape to help bind edge pieces. Also use it on countertop seams, embedded in thinset that fills the gaps between panels.

TILE TIP: Take the time to lock together cabinet components with adhesive and screws and to fasten them securely to wall studs.

Making a Sink Cutout

There are several different types of sink installations. You can mount some sinks underneath a counter and trim the edge of the opening with tile. An even more complicated option is to set the sink flush by cutting a rabbet or groove in the surrounding substrate and tiling over the lip of the sink. Both options are quite complicated and are generally taxing for do-it-yourselfers. A better approach is to tile up to the cutout and mount a self-rimming sink on the counter. It has a lip that rests on top of the tile and is the easiest to insall.

In any case, you need to make room for the sink in the plywood and cement backer board. Many sinks come with paper templates. But you can also use the sink itself (turned upside down) to draw the outline. Then measure in from the lip to draw your cut line. If you have problems centering the cutout, measure under the counter to find the center, and drive a nail up through the plywood to mark the spot.

Drill a starter hole for the blade, and cut the plywood using a saber saw. Then lay the membrane, and comb out a bed of thinset with a notched trowel to embed the cement backer board.

On sink cutouts, it's possible but extremely time-consuming to make a large, carefully shaped hole in backer board to match the plywood cutout below. Instead, run full sheets to the sides of the sink, and fill in front and back with narrow strips of backer board, leaving about a ⅛-inch gap at the seams.

Sink Cutouts

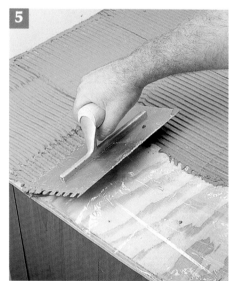

Supporting the Cutout

When you cut a sink opening in ¾-inch-thick plywood, the surrounding wood will support the cut for most of the job. But as your saw heads back to the starting point, the cutout section will start to sag. The blade may bind, and the cut piece may tear before you finish the cut.

Solve these problems with a temporary cleat. It should be long enough to cover the cut section plus an inch or so on each side. Two screws will hold the cut section to the cleat, and the ends of the cleat will hold the cutout flush with the counter.

A temporary cleat keeps the sink cutout from falling and causing a ragged break.

1. Measure carefully to center the cutout. Remember to figure only interior, front-to-back cabinet space where the sink will be housed.

2. Use a template with a framing square to position the cutout. If you trace the sink outline, measure in from the lip overhang to mark the actual cut line.

3. Although some saber saws are capable of a plunge cut, it's best to drill a starter hole. Make sure the hole is just inside your cut line.

4. Follow the cut line, working slowly at corners where you rotate the saw. Support the cutout below or install a top cleat as you finish the cut.

5. Lay a moisture membrane such as 4-mil polyethylene over the plywood. Then trowel on a bed of thinset adhesive using a notched trowel.

6. Install sheets of cement backer board up to the edges of the cutout with corrosion-resistant screws. Add narrow strips front and back.

7. Fill the ⅛-in. gaps between backer board panels with thinset, and embed a layer of fiberglass mesh tape over all the panel seams.

TILE TIP: Be sure that the cutout location leaves enough room to run supply pipes between the sink and the back of the cabinet.

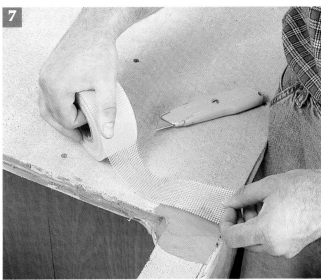

Laying the Field Tiles

If you install a new countertop tailored to the size of the field tiles and edging pieces, you should be able to snap guidelines to center up the field and another line to mark your edging tiles. If the counter will include a row of partial tiles, make a dry run with tiles and spacers to determine the best layout.

Try to minimize the number of cuts, but be sure to account for the width of your trim tiles, including all grout joints. If you plan to have a wood edging, butt the whole tiles up to the front edge of the counter surface. Always work from the front of the counter using full edge pieces next to full tiles, and let partial tiles run along the backsplash.

Establishing Working Lines

If you are tiling a rectangular countertop, find and mark the center of the front edge of the countertop. If the counter includes a sink, use it as the center so you will have a symmetrical layout around the rim. If the countertop is open at both ends, adjust the tiles so that cut tiles at each end are equal in width. If the cut tiles are much less than half a tile wide, shift the row of tiles by half a tile width, or adjust the grout joint width.

If the counter is open at only one end, lay out the tiles with full tiles along the open end and cut tiles along the wall at the opposite end. On an island counter, plan the layout with equal border tiles around all the edges.

For an L-shaped countertop, position a tile at the inside corner of the L, and pencil around the edges to mark the starting point. Because this point cannot be adjusted, you may have to cut tiles to fit exposed edges. L-shaped countertops with corner sinks usually involve odd cuts of

tile. In such cases, it is best to start with full tiles at the ends of each leg of the top and work toward the sink opening. With so many options, you can see how important it is to test your plan with a dry run.

Once you have determined the best layout, remove all the dry-laid tiles from the countertop. You can lay field tiles to a line or tack a straight 1×2 guide strip along the front of the countertop. If you are using V-caps or similar trim tiles along exposed edges, mark a line to allow for the width of the trim tiles, and start the field from the level line along the front of the counter.

Laying the First Course

Apply enough adhesive with a notched trowel to lay several tiles along the front edge. Lay the key tiles first (center or end tiles, depending on the layout). Press them gently but firmly in place. Continue filling in tiles on either side of the key tiles, using spacers if necessary, until you cannot fit any more whole tiles. Check tile alignment frequently with a straightedge or framing square.

Finishing the Field

Spread more adhesive, and continue laying rows of full tiles, working back to the wall as far as you can go without cutting any tiles. You'll find it easiest to stick with full tiles and finish the field before you tackle the partial tiles and the countertop edging.

On large or complex counters where it may take you a while to finish the field, stop periodically to scrape off any adhesive in the cut tile and edging areas. It's more difficult to clear after it sets up, and you need those areas clear and ready for fresh adhesive. Check the field surface with a straightedge to make sure that the tiles are even and level before continuing.

Scribing To an Uneven Wall

In some locations where you want to install tile, it may not be practical to remodel existing walls and make a corner perfectly square. Wherever surfaces don't meet in a clean, square-edged seam, one option is to scribe the joint.

The idea is to mirror the contour of one surface on another so that the two fit together. To make the contour line, use a compass. Hold the point end against the wall, and draw the tool evenly along so the pencil side of the tool leaves a mark that can guide your saw cut.

Keep the compass points aligned as you mark the contour of the wall onto the plywood.

1. Use one of the edge tiles to establish a working line for the main field of full tiles. Mark the edge piece at several points along all counter edges.

2. Snap chalk guidelines from the edges of the counters. Remember to allow for a grout joint between the field tiles and the edge tiles.

3. Spread adhesive over the backer board surface using a notched trowel.

4. Embed the first rows of field tiles along your guidelines. Periodically check the alignment of grout seams with a framing square.

5. Work your way along the counter to set all the full-size tiles. Check the surface with a straightedge.

1. To mark a partial tile, set a full tile so that it overlaps one of the field tiles and butts against the wall or backsplash. Mark where the two tiles meet.

2. Use a snap cutter to score the tile surface, and snap it on your mark. Remember to allow space for grout joints between tiles.

3. Use a notched trowel to continue the adhesive bed beyond the field tiles. First scrape off any dry adhesive spread when you set the field.

4. Embed partial tiles in the adhesive with firm pressure. You may want to use a straightedge to be sure the cut tiles are flush with the field.

5. Butter the backs of V-cap or other edge pieces with

adhesive. Fiberglass mesh tape on the counter edges will improve the bond.

6. Set the edge tiles to align with the grout joints of the field tiles. Work the edging pieces slightly side to side to embed them firmly.

7. To make an inside corner out of straight edging tiles, cut them at a 45 deg. angle to make a miter joint, allowing for a grout seam.

8. Set the second mitered corner piece firmly in place. If adhesive bulges out and fills the seam, clear the excess to make room for grout.

TILE TIP: If you can't order shaped inside corner pieces, cut mitered sections using a wet saw.

Partial Tile and Edging

If your installation is square, you can make all the partial tiles the same size. But it's wise to check at several points along the field tiles to see whether you need to make slight adjustments. In that case, number the tiles on the back so that you install the unique sizes in the right order. As always, wear goggles or safety glasses when cutting tiles. But if you are new to tiling, measure each tile before you cut it. This process is more time consuming, but you are less likely to make an error this way.

Overlap Measurings
There are two easy ways to make overlap measurements. In a straightforward situation where you are using plain tiles in a layout with square boundaries, use one tile. Set it in position and mark the cut line, allowing for grout and caulk seams. On more complex layouts, set one full tile on top of the adjacent field tile, and another tile on that one, but moved forward to gauge the distance to the wall. Mark the offset on the tile below, allowing for seams. Then cut and set the tile with the cut edge facing the wall. If the space is narrow, apply adhesive to the back of the tile.

Cutting Around a Sink
Some flush-mounted or inset sinks require curved cuts in all the surrounding tile. Most do-it-yourselfers will find these installations both taxing and very time-consuming. Instead of tiling to the sink, consider the more practical alternative of setting tiles up to the sink cutout and covering the edges with the lip of a self-rimming sink. This way you may be able to make most or all of the trim cuts with a snap cutter, creating a rough outline covered by the sink lip. That's a lot easier than using a nipper to cut row after row of precisely curved tiles.

Installing Edge Tiles
If you used a wood guide to align the field tiles, remove it, and clear any excess adhesive. Fiberglass mesh tape will help adhesive stick to the counter edge, but most people find that it helps to butter the edge tiles before setting them in place.

On L-shaped counters, you normally should begin at the inside corner with a curved piece. Many tile sets are available with molded inside and outside corners. Another option is to cut 45-degree angles on two straight pieces to create miter joints at the corners. Measure these cuts carefully. To maintain grout spacing, you need to align the end of the miter with the corner of the adjacent field tile.

Installing a Backsplash

There are several ways to build a backsplash. In a dry area, you can simply adhere the tiles to the wall. In wet areas, it's wiser to provide the same kind of protection you give the countertop by installing backer board. Depending on the size of the tile, you may want to install backer board only, to leave a narrow top edge. You can build a thicker backsplash with plywood and backer board (like most counters), and install a larger cap piece.

Installing Backer Board

On installations with just backer board, start by scoring and snapping a sheet to a height that will work with full tile and a top row of cap tiles. In almost all cases (unless there is a window or cabinet in the way), you should not have to use partial tiles on a backsplash. You can spread thinset on the wall, but it's easier to apply an even coat on the back of the backer board. After you set the panel firmly in place, secure it with corrosion-resistant screws driven into the studs. If the wall isn't flat, driving screws could deform the backer board. You can build a more stable surface by installing plywood and backer board.

Installing Plywood

If you're installing a new plywood counter, it's easy to join it to a solid plywood backsplash and set both pieces in place at the same time. This approach provides a very solid connection along the key seam where the counter joins the wall. You can join the backsplash to the counter

Making a Backsplash Counter

with glue and screws and take the extra step of sealing the seam with a liberal bead of silicone. If any moisture gets through the tile, this waterproof seam can prevent the backsplash from separating.

Installing Plywood and Backer Board
This is the system used for maximum durability on wet-area counters. It also provides a solid and water-resistant base for a backsplash. If you install the counter and back-splash as a connected unit, you can coat the back of the backer board or the face of the plywood before screwing the layer of backer board in place. The double layer backsplash will be very rigid.

Treat the exposed edges of plywood and backer board on the backsplash the way you treat them on the edge of the counter. Wrap them in fiberglass mesh tape before installing the cap trim.

Planning Backsplash Tile
You can use tile with a cove base on the first course of backsplash tile if you have allowed room for the curved base with the counter tiles. If tiles in the last row on the counter are cut, the joint will look better if you cover the cut edges with full tiles on the backsplash. But be sure to leave a full-size seam.

You can finish the top course of a backsplash with bull-nose tiles or V-cap-style trim tiles that wrap over the top edge. Another option is to extend the backsplash up the wall to the bottom edge of a cabinet. You can trim an extended backsplash with tile or wood trim.

---

1. Rip strips of plywood about 3 in. wide to reinforce the edges of the counter. If you don't have a table saw, use a circular saw with a guide.

2. Cut the strips to fit along the counter edges and where the counter crosses cabinet framing. Secure the strips with glue and screws.

3. Apply a liberal bead of silicone caulk to the backsplash panel where it will join the counter. Use enough to ooze out of the seam.

4. Hold the backsplash panel to the counter with clamps. You can use a square to align the pieces before fully tightening the clamps.

5. Predrill through the backsplash panel into the reinforced plywood counter. Use a combination bit to make a countersink at the same time.

6. Drive screws about every 6 in. to secure the backsplash. The pressure should squeeze the caulk into a gasket that waterproofs the seam.

7. Once the caulk sets up, peel away the excess, trimming where necessary. Then you can install the counter with the backsplash attached.

TILE TIP: A rigid joint between the counter and the backsplash can help to reduce cracking in grout seams.

One Tile and Cap

The easiest and quickest installation uses the same basic grid as the countertop tiles, and simply extends the grid one course onto the wall. Remember to leave a standard-width seam between the backsplash and the counter. Where you may get some movement between the two components, use caulk in this joint instead of grout.

Dry-Area Prep Work. In dry areas you can apply tile adhesive directly to the drywall and set the tile in place.

Wet-Area Prep Work. In wet areas, cut backer board to fit the tile and cap, comb the back of the panel with thinset, and screw with corrosion-resistant fasteners to the wall studs.

Use a notched trowel to spread adhesive from the counter to a top guideline on the wall. You can add tape to keep a clean line.

Multiple Rows and Cap

Use multiple rows of tile or combinations of sizes and shapes that create a decorative accent for the countertop. Some tiles are sold in decorative sets, such as a group of four pretrimmed tiles designed to fit around a center medallion.

Color Contrast. If you change color between the countertop and the backsplash, maintain the same grout spacing to tie the areas together. Create a more decorative look by using contrasting colors within the backsplash grid—for example, by matching the counter color with the medallion tile.

Spacing. If tiles tend to sag on the adhesive, use temporary spacers to maintain spacing.

Install pattern sets, pretrimmed for insert tiles, to create a more decorative backsplash. Inserts have to be centered to maintain grout spacing.

Multiple Trim Strips

When you begin to combine basic elements, such as single rows and tile sets with accents, you can create many variations. You can add contrasting colors to the mix and decorative tiles with an embossed pattern or picture. More complex layouts call for careful planning before installation.

Dry Layout. Test your design with a dry layout. You can temporarily tape sample pieces to a board so that you can see how the design looks on the wall.

Staggering Joints. Lining up vertical grout seams on a large backsplash emphasizes height. Offsetting intermediate trim strips so they bridge the seams between full tiles emphasizes width.

Intermediate trim strips separate different design elements on a backsplash wall. They also tie together different colors and shapes.

2 Set the row of backsplash tiles into the adhesive, but leave a standard seam along the bottom. You may need spacers to keep the tiles from sagging.

3 Cover the top edges of full backsplash tiles with a cap tile. Another option is to use tile with a finished, bullnose edge on top.

2 Press pattern insets into place by hand. You may want to use a straightedge to make sure they are flush with the surrounding tiles.

3 A larger backsplash with a more complex pattern can support a larger, S-shaped cap. You also can make caps from cut sections of bullnose tiles.

2 Horizontal trim strips provide a secondary baseline to support a row of decorative tiles with different colors and patterns.

3 When you combine different design elements, it generally looks best to use narrow trim strips in the pattern and wide trim on the cap.

Finishing a Backsplash

In most cases, you should allow the tile adhesive to set for an hour or two. (Check the manufacturer's recommendations.) If you grout too soon, some of the tiles could shift out of position. Remove tile spacers, and use a damp cloth to clean any adhesive off the tile surface. Also, check for adhesive buildup in the joints that could get in the way of grout, and use a screwdriver or narrow chisel to scrape it away.

Generally, you need to allow the adhesive to cure for at least 24 hours before grouting. If you have used unglazed tiles, coat them before grouting with a sealant recommended by the tile manufacturer. Be sure that the sealer has cured fully before applying the grout.

Applying the Grout

Mix the grout according to the manufacturer's instructions, and apply it with a rubber float or squeegee, working diagonally across the joints. You'll need to make several passes to pack the grout firmly into every joint and eliminate air bubbles.

When the grout becomes firm, use a damp sponge or a squeegee to remove excess from the tile surface. Then shape the grout joints using a striking tool. (A toothbrush handle, spoon, or something similar will work.) Clean off the tiles again with a damp sponge. Then wipe away the final haze with a clean, damp cloth. In most cases, the grout will take several days to harden completely. Then you may want to protect the seams by applying a grout sealer.

Grouting and Sealing

Use the backsplash area as a chance to add a bold design statement to your kitchen. Backsplashes are small areas that can provide a much needed shot of color or texture in kitchens where the cabinetry is a neutral color. And because it is a small space, it may make sense to invest in unusual or hand-painted tiles.

Blue tiles match the glasses on display in these cabinets. A thin contrasting border enhances the overall design.

1. Check the seams for adhesive that can mound up when you maneuver tiles into place. Remove it with a narrow chisel or screwdriver.

2. Mix the grout to a mudlike consistency (according to manufacturer's recommendations), and load it onto a rubber float.

3. Work the float on a diagonal to the tile joints to fill the seams. If you sweep the float upward, excess grout will fall back on the float.

4. To save cleanup time later on, you can use a squeegee or a damp rag to clear away excess grout from the tile surfaces.

5. If the grout is not uniform in the seams, you can strike the joints using a narrow, slightly rounded object, such as the handle of a toothbrush.

6. Wipe down the wall with a clean, damp sponge, rinsing regularly. After each cleaning (you'll need more than one) there will be less of a surface haze.

7. After polishing the wall with a soft cloth to remove the final haze, you can protect grout in wet areas by applying a liquid silicone sealer.

TILE TIP: Work your float on a diagonal from low to high so that excess grout falls back on the float.

tubs & showers

FEW MATERIALS ARE AS SUITABLE for showers and tub surrounds as tile. Smooth, highly glazed tiles are easy to clean, and the glaze can stand up to abrasive and chemical cleaners. If you are tiling a shower floor, select a vitreous or impervious glazed tile with a slip-resistant surface. Because a tub surround or shower enclosure is subjected to water and steam, both the tile and backing must be watertight. For maximum protection against seepage, you need a water-resistant adhesive such as latex thinset. Some grouts contain additives that help prevent the growth of mildew, which can be a chronic problem in poorly ventilated bathrooms.

Where tile joins a tub, you need the stability and water resistance of cement-based backer board on the surrounding walls. You also need to make a solid tub installation. If you use a fiberglass or acrylic unit, reduce flexing (which can open tile seams) by packing the base in a supporting material of quick-drying plaster. With tubs or spas that rest on tiled platforms, it's important to build a substantial supporting floor for the unit.

Preparing the Site

In a new house or addition, you can prepare tub and shower enclosures that are square and level, and build in modern, watertight substrates. In an existing house, the first step often is to remove old tile and the thick bed of mortar beneath it. This is always messy and sometimes

potentially dangerous, so you should wear safety goggles, a dust mask, work gloves, and a heavy long-sleeved shirt as you demolish old wall surfaces.

Removing Old Tile

To start, protect the work area with sheets of plywood and a tarp or drop cloth. Use a sledgehammer and cold chisel to remove the tiles, starting from the top course and working downward. You may want to place a large bucket directly beneath the tiles to catch them. If the tiles are set in mortar, you also may need to snip through reinforcing mesh to release chunks from the wall. When you remove tiles from drywall, some of the paper facing usually tears off, exposing the gypsum core. Once this happens, either remove the panel or install another layer of backing material over it. If you find plaster or conventional drywall around a tub or shower, cover it or replace it with backer board.

Fixtures

In most cases, you need the rough plumbing in place before you start a tile installation. If you're installing a prefabricated shower pan that comes with a drain hole, you may want to set it in place and mark the subfloor first. That way you can adjust the plumbing connections a bit to get a perfect fit. More often, walls have short pipe stems protruding. You can tile close to them without making exact cuts because the pipes are covered by escutcheon plates. If you're re-tiling an area, remove handles and trim pieces, and protect threaded ends during the work.

Removing Old Tile

1. If you have trouble getting started, drill a few holes in a tile using a masonry bit. The holes create a fault line that makes the tile easy to break.

2. Use a cold chisel to split off sections of tile and to chop out grout. Remember to wear safety glasses to guard against flying chips of tile.

3. Once you have an exposed edge of tile and adhesive (or mortar) to work on, use the flat end of a pry bar to pop tiles off the wall.

TILE TIP: If you find standard drywall behind old tile around a tub or shower, the best plan is to remove it and install cement-based backer board in its place.

Installing Prefab Pans

If you use a prefabricated shower pan, tiling a shower enclosure becomes a doable do-it-yourself project. You don't have to float a mortar bed on the floor that slopes down to a drain. You can tile the flat wall surfaces down to the pan without having to deal with cove tiles at the base and aligning wall joints with floor joints.

You do need to build the enclosure to suit the size of the pan. To make your planning and layout more accurate, you may want to buy the pan before framing. That way you can be sure that the unit will fit. Also, prefabricated pans generally come with a drain hole already drilled. You could do all the rough plumbing ahead of time, and hope that you have the drain at dead center of the enclosure. But it's safer to set the pan in place after the framing is done, and mark the drain location on the subfloor through the hole in the pan.

Even when you use a prefabricated pan, there are many elements to coordinate. If only one measurement is off the intended layout, such as an off-center drain line, you might have to adjust the framing and move the pan, which could throw off your tile layout on the enclosure walls. If you're considering a custom enclosure with a floated floor, remember that it will be even more complex and require more thorough planning.

Framing Support

You can use standard framing lumber and techniques to build a tub or shower enclosure. The basic frame consists

Setting a Shower Pan

of a 2×4 laid flat on the floor, studs 16 inches on center, and double 2×4s across the top of the wall. Select the straightest and driest studs possible to build your walls. Wet lumber can twist enough to disrupt tile joints even when the frame is covered with cement-based backer board.

It's important to provide adequate nailing surfaces for the backer board, so don't scrimp on lumber at the corners. If you use ½-inch backer board, remember that the thickness of the piece on one side of the corner will reduce the available nailing surface on the other.

When the pan is in place and the drain flange is attached, conduct a water test. Plug the drain and flood the pan with water to be sure that the drain seal is working. Protect the pan and drain when you tile the walls.

You can create a custom look by inserting a contrasting border and changing the size of the tile.

1. Check the enclosure to be sure the framing is square. Add extra studs if necessary to provide adequate nailing surfaces in the corners.

2. On new construction, you can mark the drain hole and run plumbing to suit. Over existing drains, you must adjust the enclosure to center the pan.

3. After removing the pan, drill a starting hole, and cut through the subfloor using a saber saw or reciprocating saw to get access to the drainpipe.

4. Set the pan in place, align the drain holes, and check for level. You need a level pan and square walls to avoid an irregular tile layout.

5. Screw or nail through the pan base flange into the studs. For extra support you can add 2x6 blocking on the flat between studs.

6. With the pan in position over the drainpipe, follow manufacturer's recommendations for installing the drain gasket.

7. Apply cement-based backer board to the studs with corrosion-resistant screws or nails. Seal and tape the seams before adding adhesive and tiling.

TILE TIP: Some pans have narrow ledges for thin surround panels. For tile and backer board, you need a pan with a deep ledge.

Floating a Shower Floor

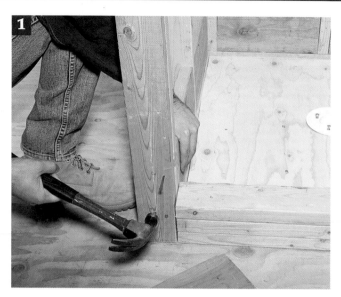

1. Build a curb across the front of the enclosure, and add blocking on the flat between the studs. Add another layer of underlayment over the subfloor.

2. Carefully measure and rough-trim the shower pan liner. Fold over extra material at the corners and secure only the top edge all around using staples.

3. Cut the membrane using a utility knife to install the drain. Most drains have two parts that you bolt together to sandwich the membrane.

4. Attach the upper drain assembly to the lower assembly using bolts. Sandwich the membrane between the assemblies in sealant beds.

5. Strike lines on the wall to create a slope to the drain of about ¼ in. per foot. Apply about half the final thickness of mortar, establishing the slope.

6. Embed galvanized reinforcing mesh in the mortar, and bend up an inch or so on the walls. The metal adds strength to the masonry base.

7. Apply the rest of the mortar, mixed to the consistency of wet sand. Use a trowel to smooth out corners and a large float to smooth the slopes.

8. Spread a layer of thinset over the hardened mortar according to the tile manufacturer's recommendations, and begin to apply the tiles.

Installing a Mortar-Bed Floor

This is one of the most difficult types of tile installations, and it's often best left to the pros. Although parts of the job are common to all tile work, a few areas are unfamiliar to do-it-yourselfers.

Framing Details

There are three keys to this part of the project. First, install blocking between the surrounding joists to provide continuous support for the base. Make the blocking several inches higher than the mortar bed so that you can run the membrane up the wall and under the bottom edge of the backer board.

Second, install a wood curb made of three 2×4s to form the front of the shower base. You can also form the curb space and pour in reinforced mortar as an extension of the floor. But this approach is more difficult, and you have no way to make the slight adjustments needed to keep the tile layout symmetrical.

Third, add extra framing to make the floor absolutely rigid. It pays to double up joists under a shower (and even more so under a tub) and to use ¾-inch exterior-grade plywood for the underlayment.

Flexible Membranes

You can make a waterproof pan out of lead, copper, and other materials. But the most modern and practical material is a heavy, flexible membrane made of chlorinated polyethylene (CPE) or polyvinyl chloride (PVC). It is flexible enough to fold snugly into corners. Many suppliers also provide shaped patches to provide extra waterproofing at complex joints. Before tiling, seal the drain and fill the pan with water for 24 hours to test for leaks.

Drain Fixtures

Standard fixture drains have a single collar on the surface (usually set in silicone sealant) that threads onto the rough plumbing to finish and seal the drain area. Drains in tiled showers are different. A typical unit has three separate parts. The lower flange connects to the drainpipe and includes bolt holes for the upper flange. Typically, the top of the lower flange rests flush with the subfloor. You cut the flexible membrane to allow drainage, and clamp down its edges in sealant beds by bolting on the upper flange. This part has a stem that rises to the level of your mortar and weep holes to drain any moisture in the mortar bed. It is topped by a finished chrome screen.

Setting Tub and Shower Tile

Basic installation is the same on shower walls as it is on other walls. Because of the wet conditions, however, there is a difference in the use of substrates.

Greenboard and Backer Board

On dry-area walls, you can tile directly over standard wallboard. In showers, you need cement-based backer board or specially treated, water-resistant drywall, generally called greenboard.

Backer board is the best choice because it will not deteriorate when wet, while greenboard eventually may soften and give way. But you should check local building codes for details. Many now require a waterproof membrane between the studs and backing material.

Working Lines. Establish your vertical and horizontal working lines on the back wall because it is the most visible. Then project the horizontal lines to the adjoining walls, and center vertical working lines on each wall to be tiled. Ideally, you want a course of full tiles around the shower pan, leaving a gap for mildew-resistant silicone,

acrylic, or latex tub-and-tile caulk to allow for expansion and contraction. Because you will be working in a small area, tile the back wall first. Then fill in the sidewalls, stub walls, and threshold. This way you're not likely to disturb tiles that have already been set.

The Main Vertical Line. Center the vertical working line on the back wall. Then establish the vertical lines on the side walls. The installation will look best if the cut tiles on the inside corners of the end walls are equal in width to those on the back wall. If you are tiling a shower enclosure with stub walls, plan on cutting tiles to fit around the threshold to maintain continuous grout lines. If possible, adjust the layout lines to avoid extremely narrow-cut tiles around the opening.

The Main Horizontal Line. If the tub or shower pan is level to within ⅛ inch, locate the horizontal working line by leveling from the high point of the rim. Measure up the wall the width of one whole tile, plus enough room for a grout joint on top and a caulk joint next to the pan. A slight variation in the gap between the rim and first course of tiles will not be noticeable after it is caulked.

Cover areas that will get wet, such as shower walls and tub surrounds, with cement backer board before tiling.

Applying Adhesive

Apply adhesive on the surface using the straight side of your trowel to spread the mix and the notched side to comb it out into even ribs.

To keep the job moving smoothly, complete one full wall before starting on the next. If you apply adhesive to more than one wall before setting the tiles, the adhesive may start to set up or skin over. To see how much working time you have, check the adhesive label. If you are covering a small area of the wall, it is often possible to cover the entire surface with adhesive and lay the tiles before the adhesive sets up or loses its tack. On larger surfaces, fill in small sections at a time.

Installing Tile Supports

Standard working procedure is to install the second course first and the first course last. This allows you to work to a dead level line even if the shower pan lip is slightly out of level. Later on you can go back to the first course and set the tiles with a grout space above and a caulk space below.

To keep the field of tiles from sagging as you work, you may want to install a batten (a straight-edged strip of plywood as in Step 5 or a 1×2) or a row of nails along the level working line. Once the field tiles are set, remove the batten and set the first course of tiles.

Before you start setting tiles, it pays to double-check the space below the working line. Remember that you need to allow for a grout line between the first and second course and at least ⅛ in. for a caulked seam along the shower pan.

Tiling Sequence

Start by laying the first tiles against the vertical layout line, and work the field out to each corner. As always, it's wise to make periodic checks using a straightedge and a spirit level to be sure that the tile grid is still running square with the original layout lines.

Pay particular attention to the grout lines as you work. Unlike tiles you lay on floors and counters, wall tiles can sometimes sag on the adhesive and close up the grout seams. You can solve this problem by starting the field on a row of temporary nails or a batten, and supporting each new course with spacers.

When the main field is finished, cut and add edge pieces as needed. Allow the tile adhesive to set according to manufacturer's directions. Then you can come back and install the grout.

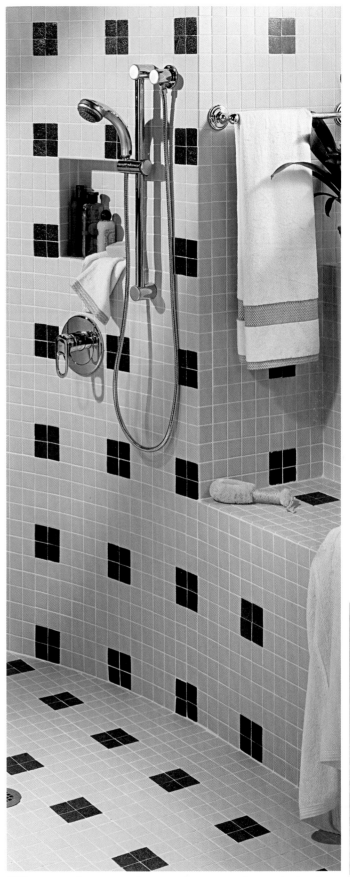

When you frame custom enclosures, plan seats, inset shelves, and other features to accommodate full tiles.

1. Measure the back wall of the enclosure to find the center. Be sure to do
a test layout to see how partial tiles will fall in the corners.

2. Use a chalk-line box to snap the main vertical working line on the back of the enclosure. That wall is important because it is the most visible.

3. Check using a level to find the high point, and then measure up one full tile plus a grout joint at the top and bottom of the tile.

4. Make level marks, and snap the horizontal working line around the enclosure. If the base isn't exactly level, the discrepancy will be in the grout joint.

5. To support the field tiles and prevent sagging, you can install a temporary plywood batten with screws driven into the enclosure studs.

6. Use a notched trowel to spread adhesive up to the lines. For the best bond, spread adhesive using the flat edge first.

7. Rake back across the adhesive with the notched edge of the trowel. The adhesive should have a recommended notch size.

8. Set full tiles along the horizontal working line, using spacers to maintain even grout seams. You can complete full rows or work a pyramid shape.

9. Set a full tile on the last tile in the main field to mark the corner pieces, allowing for a grout seam in the corner. Trim them using a snap cutter.

10. Rake out adhesive for the bottom row, and set the tiles. Use temporary spacers or tape to keep the tiles centered.

11. When the adhesive sets up (usually overnight), you can use a rubber float to spread grout into the seams.

TILE TIP: Plan the layout so that shower doors will mount over full tiles.

Installing Accessories

Many fiberglass and acrylic showers are manufactured with recessed soap dishes, grab bars, and small corner seats already molded in. In a custom-tiled shower, of course, you have to install these features yourself.

Soap Dishes and Grab Bars

There are two ways to handle these fixtures. One is to tile the wall completely and drill through the tile to surface-mount the accessories using screws. The other, which generally looks better, is to use dish and towel-bar fixtures that match the tile color and grid. Because their mounting areas are multiples of the full tiles, you can add them after you set the field tiles without cutting or trim-

ming. Note that recessed dishes may require some extra work on the framing and substrate before you start tiling.

You can adhere soap dishes with thinset adhesive applied to the wall and buttered on the back of the dish. For safety, locate dish fixtures where they will not be used as handholds. Grab bars generally require strong fittings that are attached to wall studs behind the tile substrate.

Shower Seats

You can buy prefinished shower seats or forms that you can tile to blend in with the enclosure. These have a seat frame that you mount on the supporting studs. Then you add adhesive, tile, and grout the way you do on the walls.

Installing a Soap Dish

1. Scrape off any dried adhesive residue from the full tiles surrounding the opening, and spread thinset adhesive on the wall.

2. Use a small trowel to butter the back of the soap dish with adhesive. Then press the dish into place and align it with the adjacent tiles.

3. Maintain pressure on the dish as the adhesive sets by applying two long strips of masking tape across the front edge of the dish.

TILE TIP: Although some soap dishes have a built-in bar (intended for a washcloth), they are not designed to withstand the weight of a person. It's wise to use dishes without a bar.

Recessed Soap Dishes

A recessed soap dish is a convenient extra that you can build into your tile job. Some units require a small 2x4 frame to support the bottom and the sides of the dish within the wall. The easiest option is to add a surface-mounted dish. It has a lip that rests on the surrounding tile. You also can add a ceramic dish by making an access hole in the substrate. Use thinset adhesive to fasten a scrap piece of membrane to the inside of the framed support, spread about 1/16 inch of thinset adhesive on the back of the dish, and press it into place.

To mount a recessed soap dish, an extra piece of blocking is needed between studs. Plan for this before you begin installing tile.

Installing a Grab Bar

1. Locate wall studs, generally 16 in. on center. Apply masking tape to the surface of the tile, and drill using a masonry or glass-cutting bit.

2. You may not be able to hit a stud with every fastener. In such cases use heavy-duty hollow-wall anchors or toggle bolts.

3. Tighten all fasteners until the bar does not move when force is applied to it. Be careful not to overtighten the screws and crack the tile.

TILE TIP: For maximum safety, don't rely on anchors in drywall or backer board. Fasten bar mounts directly to wall studs.

specialty tiling

Fireplaces

Whether you are building a new fireplace or remodeling an existing unit, you can use ceramic tile to make an elegant, fire-safe covering for the hearth and fireplace face wall. You can tile the hearth only, the hearth and firebox surround, or add a single row of decorative tiles around the fireplace opening as an accent. In all cases, check local building codes, and be sure that you make a fire-safe installation.

Selecting Materials

Around a fireplace, use tile that is resistant to both heat and the impact of an accidentally dropped log. Heavy-duty quarry tiles, pavers, or glazed floor tiles are all good choices. If the manufacturer offers more than one thickness, go with the beefier size. If you are tiling over concrete, brick, or other masonry, use nonflammable heat-resistant mortar, such as a dry-set cement. Do not use organic mastics. If you are tiling over an existing wood floor, it's wise to install at least one layer of cement-based backer board. Remember that on installations that extend an existing hearth or add a new one, you may need to strengthen the subfloor.

Hearth Design

The hearth on the floor in front of a fireplace should be covered with tile, brick, or other masonry material that can stand up to sparks and embers. You can cut the masonry area out of the finished floor to make a tiled hearth flush with the surrounding floor. But it's easier to leave the existing wood in place and create a slightly raised hearth by applying backer board and trimming the edges. It generally looks best to extend the hearth at least a tile or two on each side of the opening. Typically, the hearth rests on a full foundation or a poured concrete slab about 4 inches thick supported by extra framing and hardware. The hearth generally extends at least 16 inches out and 8 inches on each side of the firebox. If the existing hearth isn't up to code, it's a good idea to bring it up to code before tiling.

Face-Wall Design

On masonry fireplaces, you can set tiles in a bed of mortar spread over lath attached to the existing brick, block, or stone. With prefab metal fireplaces, you should be able to build a surround to suit the tile grid and cover the framed enclosure with cement-based backer board. Use a heat-resistant epoxy mortar to apply tile to metal and a heat-resistant cement mortar on masonry surfaces.

Setting the Tiles

You can set ceramic tile over an existing masonry hearth if the surface is relatively flat. Rigidity is usually not a problem with masonry. If you are dealing with a rough surface, a thick bond coat of mortar will fill mortar joints and provide a suitable surface for the tile. Grind down any high spots, and clean the surface thoroughly to remove soot or dirt. Then apply a bond coat to fill in irregularities. When the bond coat dries, make your layout lines, and apply a second coat of mortar to set the tiles according to the manufacturer's instructions.

To tile either a flush or raised hearth, start by tiling the front with full tiles. It pays to make a test fit in advance, accounting for tile and grout joints. After the tiles have set up, grout the joints, and if the hearth is raised, add trim. Caulk the seam between the tile and trim and between the wall and the hearth.

A variety of tile shapes combine to trim an unusual-shaped opening and provide the intricate appearance normally associated with a carved wooden surround.

1. Locate the midpoint of the opening, and mark a line to center the hearth. Generally, hearths should be at least 16 in. deep.

2. Score and snap a sheet of backer board, and set it in a bed of thinset mortar. Leave a gap for caulking next to the fireplace, and secure using screws.

3. Snap layout lines for your tile, and rake out a bed of thinset over the backer board using the notched edge of your trowel.

4. On a hearth, you may want to start with a dry layout to be sure the tiles will fit. Embed the cut tiles first, and follow with full tiles and edging.

5. Add trim around the edges of the hearth. Wood strips with mitered corners make a nice transition between a wood floor and a tiled hearth.

TILE TIP: To strengthen a floor without adding double layers of plywood or backer board, which will raise the hearth, you can double up the supporting joists. This is a good option if the room beneath the one with the hearth is unfinished, such as a basement or crawl space. Select joist lumber that is the same dimension as the original framing; install the new joist against the original, securing the lumber to the rim joists; connect the new and old joists by using construction adhesive and screws.

1. Use a layout stick to plan the installation and prepare for a test fit. Be sure to size cut tiles on each side of the opening so that they match.

2. Use a notched trowel to rake out a bed of thinset adhesive over the substrate, and set full tiles (or trim strip tiles) around the fireplace opening.

3. Once the tile is securely set, generally overnight, use a float to grout the joints. Clean off the dried grout haze using a damp sponge.

TILE TIP: Adjust grout joints as needed to line up full tiles around the fireplace opening.

Tiling a Fireplace Face

There is no one correct way to tile the face of a fireplace, because there are so many different types of installations. Over rough brick, for example, you might need to add layers of metal lath and mortar to create a smooth setting bed. Over a zero-clearance prefab unit with walls that never get very hot, you might frame-in the face and install a layer of cement-based backer board.

Generally you can follow the same approach as you do tiling walls. The main difference, of course, is that most installations require heat-resistant materials such as epoxy-based mortar to apply tile to metal, and cement-based mortar over masonry surfaces or backer board. Be sure you check the installation against local codes, which are strict when it comes to fire safety.

A common stumbling block on fireplace installations (and walls, too) is keeping tiles from sagging until they set. One solution is to install a row of temporary support nails or a wooden batten along the top of where you'll set the bottom row. (See pages 60–61 and 86–87.) Once the main tiles have set, you can remove the support and secure the bottom row of tiles by taping them to the set tiles above. Another option, especially for traditional fireplaces, is to build a temporary wood trestle to bridge the firebox opening and support the tiles.

On many prefab units, you can bring the tile right to the built-in lip around the fireplace opening. On masonry fireplaces, you need to trim the edge using bullnose tile or decorative tile strips. Be sure to make a test layout starting with full tiles around the opening so you can see where partial tiles may be needed.

Stairs

It is possible to tile both stair treads—the part you step on—and stair risers—the vertical panel between treads. But it can be difficult for do-it-yourselfers to match the design of wood steps and create an overhang at each tread. The more doable and often better-looking project is to use tile on the risers only as a decorative feature, and stick with traditional wood planks with an overhang on the treads.

If you want to tile the treads, consider ordering special stair-tread tiles that come with a rounded nosing to project slightly past the front edge of the riser. Without getting too technical about it, this design does make a safer step that's easier to negotiate than a right-angle box

shape with no overhang, and it looks better.

Another option is to use large, unglazed quarry or paver tiles that are often used for the treads on outdoor steps. You may be able to create a small tread overhang with tile and supporting trim strips. You can't project a standard floor tile past the riser without support because it is too likely to crack.

Whatever tile you select for the treads should be slip-resistant and durable enough to withstand heavy foot traffic. Tiles for risers, on the other hand, can be relatively thin glazed wall tiles. You can install them in a continuous band across the riser or add just one accent tile in the center of the riser.

Design Considerations

Most stairs are strong enough to support tile because they are designed to support people. But some treads do flex slightly, which is just enough to disrupt tile grout and lead to repair problems and possible safety hazards. It's difficult to detect minimal flexing, although the sound of squeaking wood is a sure sign that stair components are moving. On an existing staircase with this problem, you can take several approaches.

The most drastic improvement is to add a center stringer. This effectively cuts the span of each tread and riser in half, providing twice as much support. But you can also screw steel angle brackets to treads and risers, insert wooden wedges, and add long wood screws to create a more secure connection between the stairs and supporting walls. Another option is to install wooden blocks with glue and screws along the seams between treads and risers at midspan where they are weakest and most likely to flex.

Of course, it's possible to make these improvements only if you have access from below to the stair framing or if you remove a tread. But if you are planning to cover treads and risers with tile, you can drive screws through exposed surfaces to tighten up the structure. If you do this, it's wise to countersink the holes so that screwheads are flush and cannot crack the tiles.

If you are tiling over concrete steps (a project that is more likely outside than inside), clean the masonry surfaces to improve adhesion, and repair any cracks or other faults that could create weak spots under the tile. If you are building a new set of wooden steps for tiling, provide a suitable substrate such as exterior-grade ¾-inch plywood. On deep treads you can use two layers of the plywood to prevent flexing as long as you stay within code limits for riser and tread dimensions. You can also guard against cracking by using a flexible caulk along the seam between tread tiles and riser tiles.

You can combine heavy-duty tread tiles that have a built-in nosing with thinner, more decorative tiles on the risers.

Tiling Stairs

1. You can strengthen stairs with closed framing by driving screws at an angle through the face of the riser and into the tread.

2. To improve the adhesive bond on risers, scrape off old paint, and sand down any rough spots using medium-grit paper.

3. Clean up any sanding dust that you created. Protect the treads from tile ahesive by applying painter's tape where necessary. Do a test fit with full tiles ahead of time to plan any partial cuts. Use a small notched spreader to cover the riser with adhesive.

4. Snip off the bottom of a spacer so you can insert it between the tile and the tread, creating space for the caulk joint and to keep the tiles from sagging. You can also use finishing nails for this purpose.

5. Once the tile has set, grout the vertical seams, and wipe away the final grout haze. Use flexible caulk in the tread seams.

TILE TIP: Use a flexible caulk to fill the seam between the riser and the tread rather than grout. Grout will crack if the tread flexes or expands and contracts.

Tiling Existing Concrete

If you're starting from scratch, you can pour a solid slab to support the tile. If you have a solid slab already, you'll generally need to do only a little cleaning and touch-up work. But you also can use tile to cover up surface cracks and other problems in an older patio, and let the existing masonry serve as a foundation.

If the slab is badly fractured, you may have to pour new concrete footings and refinish the surface. It's a lot of work, but it makes sense when compared with paying someone to break up the old patio and cart it away.

If the slab is covered with surface cracks but is still flat and stable, it is a good candidate for pouring a thin cover slab. If parts of the slab are tilting in different directions and bobbing up and down each season like slow-motion icebergs, you will have to beef up the slab support system. It's wise to consult an engineer or experienced masonry contractor about this work.

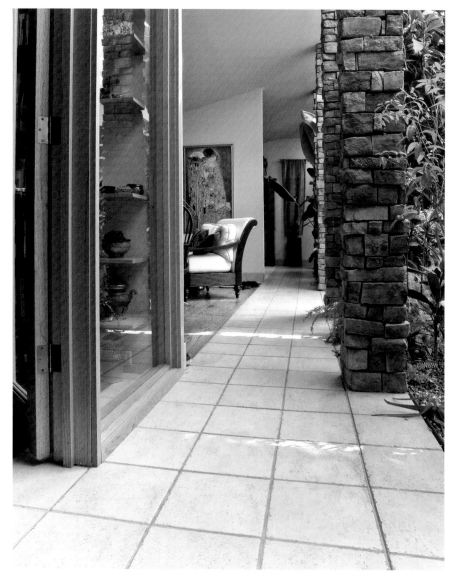

You can't expect good results patching major cracks on a slab that moves seasonally. The cracks will open again and disrupt the tile surface.

Testing the Surface

Before you clean the surface and make repairs, it's a good idea to test the concrete to see whether a curing agent was used. Some of these agents can interfere with the adhesive bond between the slab and the tile. Some surface sealers can have the same effect.

To make the test, sprinkle some water on the slab and see if it beads up or soaks in. If the water beads up, a curing agent was probably used.

To prevent a curing agent or sealer from disrupting the tile bond, you can sandblast the surface. The homeowner equivalent is pressure-washing. But you have to handle these machines with caution because a high-pressure stream of water can be strong enough to pit solid concrete. You don't generally need to use chemical removers with a high-pressure spray.

Preparing the Surface

Start by grinding down any high spots with a power grinder. To fix small cracks and chips, start by digging out the crevices using a narrow cold chisel or screwdriver. Be sure to remove any loose mortar. It's also a good idea to use a stiff brush or compressed air to clean cracks of any dirt, old leaves, or other debris.

You can use a mason's trowel to fill cracks and holes with masonry patching compound. You may also need to fill low spots with the patching compound.

If you don't pressure-wash, you can use a commercial concrete cleaner to remove any grease, wax, or other contaminants. Rinse thoroughly with water, and let the slab dry.

To prevent puddling, slope the slab slightly away from the house. You can test this easily enough by checking the slab after a heavy rain or by spraying the slab using a hose.

To correct the problem before tiling, you need to coat a thick bed of cement mortar over the entire patio, sloping it about $1/8$ inch per foot. After the mortar cures, you can set the tile with thinset mortar.

Large tiles make a handsome patio that will not rot, splinter, or provide a food source for termites.

1. Rather than fill shallow voids in the concrete, check for high spots by moving a straightedge across the slab. Mark the high spots as you proceed across the surface of the slab. Then use a power grinder with an abrasive wheel to reduce the high spots until the concrete slab is level.

2. Sweep away dirt and debris, which can interfere with tile adhesion. Pressure-washing or a blast of compressed air works well on cracks. But for flat surfaces, sweeping with a broom should be sufficient.

3. Clear loose concrete and debris from cracks. Then use a trowel to press in patching mortar. Make several passes to be sure the crack is filled. Make sure the patch is level with the surrounding area.

4. To improve the bond between the slab and the tile, clean the slab using a pressure-washer—or do it the old-fashioned way, by hand.

5. Use a garden hose to rinse the surface thoroughly and remove any traces of cleaning agents, which could interfere with the adhesive bond.

TILE TIP: Pressure-washing often can remove debris from cracks, clear loose mortar, and clean the surface in one operation.

1. The support post on this covered entryway controls the layout. You have to make sure that it falls on a seam, not in the middle of a full tile.

2. On a job like this, you may have to experiment with different test layouts. Then you can cut the first notch and move on to the main field.

3. Working back from the notched tile that aligns with the edge of the slab, snap chalk lines to guide the full-sized field tiles.

4. Measure and cut the other side of the post notch. Then trowel on thinset adhesive using a notched trowel. Set spacers at the joints.

5. As you work into the main field, rake out a larger area of thinset, and set full tiles in rows. Periodically, check for

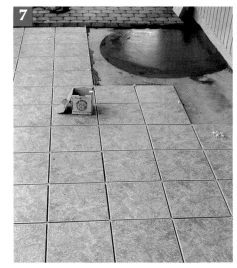

crac

G
gene
tile.
struc
builc
weal
tub,

W
affor
to se
hesiv
supp
en ar
In ex
ing fl

alignment by measuring and using a long straightedge.

6. If you encounter a low spot, fill it with a slurry of concrete patch material. Generally, it pays to test the slab using a straightedge ahead of time.

7. You can smooth the patch slurry over a low spot, but a soupy mix is almost self-leveling. Check the manufacturer's specs about hardening time.

8. Apply grout with a sponge-faced trowel or squeegee, working at a diagonal to the joints. Use flexible grout in seams against the house.

TILE TIP: Test layouts are essential on jobs with several built-in limitations such as the edge of an existing slab or a support post or other structures that interrupt the tile field.

Ro

For d
warr
or va
the til

Th
move
spots
free, :
Don't
Alway
shoul

If y
plasti
flecks
using
the tile
clean
that cc

Rem

Strong
clean
remov
remov
comm
buildu
hard-w

To
Then u
move
nary d
spot tc
If the g
and-tile

Finishing a Slab

You can have a ready-mix company spread the concrete for you—up to a point. You'll have to shovel the mix into corners, be sure that the welded wire is properly embedded, and use different trowels to cut control joints and finish the edges. All in all, pouring a slab is a job that most DIYers would be wise to turn over to a contractor.

The most difficult operation for most people is to smooth out the surface. If you are leveling a narrow patio or walkway, you can use a board wide enough to rest on top of the forms. By working the board back and forth, you can gradually fill in small voids and smooth out the surface as you move along the forms. On a larger surface, you can use a long 2×4 or other straightedge. Most pros use a large, lightweight float with a long handle. These are generally available at tool-rental shops. However you smooth the surface, don't overwork the concrete. It brings excess water to the surface and creates uneven distribution of the concrete ingredients.

Before the concrete hardens, you need to cut control joints. You may also want to check into the process of curing, which can be quite complicated. In a nutshell, this is a gradual process of hardening that provides strength and durability. If the concrete dries out too quickly, it can lose strength. If you keep the surface damp for several days, it gains strength. You can do this by misting the surface using a hose several times a day, applying a special sealer that traps moisture, or covering the wet concrete slab using plastic sheeting.

Laying the Tile

Once the concrete is cured (or repaired and cleaned if you're working on an existing slab), snap your working lines on the concrete. You can use the same approach you use for tiling floors. But if you planned ahead to accommodate full tiles in the size of your slab, the layout should be straightforward.

Trowel on the thinset adhesive using a notched trowel matched to the tile and adhesive according to manufacturer's recommendations. On an uneven slab, first you may need to apply a thin bond coat of mortar over the entire surface using a smooth trowel. Remember to check the working temperature limits of the adhesive.

Set the tiles in place, twisting slightly to embed them in the adhesive. As always, check your work frequently, using a straightedge to make sure the tiles are level and aligned. Then apply an appropriate grout as recommended by the tile manufacturer.

Routine Maintenance

Sealing Grout & Unglazed Tile

You can apply a clear sealer to the grout joints only, or to the entire floor, if you have unglazed tiles. A sealer doesn't eliminate cleaning and periodic repairs, but it does add a measure of protection against stains. You may find that some sealers darken the tile a bit in the same way that a clear coating can slightly change the hue of brick or concrete in a patio.

The drawback is that you need to reapply the sealer about every two years (or as specified by the manufacturer) to maintain protection. And before you can roll out another coating, you'll need to clean the tile and grout thoroughly and allow the floor to dry completely.

Optional Waxing

Many tile waxes and buffing compounds are available for unglazed tile floors. Some are colored to enhance the appearance of unglazed terra-cotta tiles or pavers. After cleaning the floor with a soap-free floor cleaner and rinsing thoroughly with clear water, let the surface dry, and buff out the existing wax to restore the shine. When it's time to reapply wax, you'll need to strip off any old wax, wash the floor with a mild detergent, and rinse thoroughly with clear water. Two or three light coats of wax look better than one heavy coat.

The drawback is that a buffed wax finish can make tile floors slippery. You have to decide whether the improved appearance and protection is worth the increased risk of an accidental slip or fall.

Cleaning Old Grout

1. Few specialized cleaners can match the effectiveness of straight household bleach on mold-stained grout. Test a small section on dark grout.

2. Let a puddle of bleach sit for a few minutes on the most stubborn stains. Brushing can help to dislodge deep stains in porous grout.

3. Once the grout is clean and dry, reduce further staining (and cleaning) by coating grout seams with a clear sealer.

Tile Tip: Remember that straight bleach may discolor the surface of unglazed tile. You should test a small section to see the result.

Maintaining Tub Surrounds

If you spill water on a tile counter or floor, you'll probably wipe it up. But the tile and grout around tubs and showers get soaked and stay wet on a regular basis. This makes the area difficult to keep clean and a prime candidate for a complete overhaul. (See the how-to sequence on the following pages.)

Often the most troublesome location is the seam between the wall tiles and the edges of the tub. One reason for trouble: some do-it-yourselfers grout this seam along with the rest of the tile joints instead of filling it with caulk. A liberal bead of flexible silicone caulk helps to shed water. It also bridges the gap between the wall tiles, which are subject to one set of stresses, and the tub, which is subject to another.

Seal the junction between the wall tiles and the tub surround with a flexible silicone caulk.

Removing Old Grout

1. Grout-removal attachments are typically sold as accessories for rotary-type power tools. The guide hood clamps over the chuck.

2. The hood of the attachment seats the tool on the tile, while guide nibs keep the cutter aligned with the grout seam.

3. With a grout-removal attachment, you can clean out the seams between tiles without damaging or dislodging the surrounding tiles.

TILE TIP: Be sure to adjust the guide so that the cutting bit does not dig into the sides of the tiles.

1. To scrape out damaged or deeply stained grout you can use a carpet knife, a small grout saw, or a power grout-removal tool.

2. On many older installations you need to slice off one or more layers of old caulk and clean out the seam between the tile and the tub.

3. If you need to scrub stubborn soap scum or water deposits, use a sponge or plastic pad, not steel wool, which can cause rust stains.

4. When the damaged grout is cleared and the joints are brushed clean, mix fresh grout to a workable, slightly soupy consistency.

5. Spread grout using strokes on the diagonal to the seams. Use a rubber-surfaced float for spreading and a squeegee for removing the excess.

6. When the grout sets up you can make the first of many passes using a clean, damp rag to remove extra residue and the final grout haze.

7. To create a waterproof seal between the bottom row of tiles and the tub, apply a continuous bead of a flexible, silicone-based caulk.

8. To smooth out a bead of caulk, the not-very-high-tech tool that often works best is the end of your finger dipped in soapy water.

9. To prevent water from seeping behind the plumbing fixtures and under the tiles, also apply a thin bead of caulk around the fixture edges.

10. This grout calls for wet curing. You keep it damp by misting with water several times a day. Plastic sheets help contain the moisture.

11. To protect the new grout and reduce the need for future maintenance and repairs, seal the seams using clear silicone sealer.

TILE TIP: Once the grout is cleaned (or replaced), taking the time to seal it will greatly reduce the need for more cleaning.

Digging Out Grout

You can dig out grout using a cold chisel, or cut it away using a power grout-removal tool. (See page 103.) But there are two other methods to consider. You can simply drill out the grout by making a series of holes using a masonry bit, or cut it out using a small handheld grout saw that has an abrasive edge.

Hand grout saws have both abrasive and toothed cutting blades.

Masonry bits have an extended carbide tip to cut through grout.

Fixing Broken Tiles

You can break a damaged tile into small pieces that are easy to remove. But if surrounding tiles are solidly interlocked with grout, the reverberating forces of a hammer and cold chisel are likely to cause even more damage. A better approach in many cases is to remove the grout first.

Dislodging Tiles

One way to contain the project is to use hand tools with a minimum amount of force, digging and prying instead of hammering. For example, when a piece of tile is loose, you can carve out some grout and work a screwdriver under the section that still adheres to the subfloor. If the tile is cracked but solidly set, drill a row of holes across the tile to create a fault line that will break with a few light taps. This exposes edges that you can more easily pry and lift.

If the tile is difficult to drill (even new masonry bits tend to skid on glazed surfaces) you can drill a series of small holes in the solid grout bordering the tile. The trick is to keep the bit centered and avoid damaging adjacent tiles as you drill. The holes make it easier to dig out the grout and expose the edges of the tile. If the surrounding grout is already loose, score the seams around the tile using a grout saw or utility knife, making repeated passes as needed to isolate the tile. Then use a narrow screwdriver to pry out the grout so you can work on the tile. With the grout gone, a cracked tile is easily pried up using a cold chisel or screwdriver tip.

Another approach is to use either a power grout-removing attachment on a rotary tool or a small grout saw to clear away the grout. Hand-held rotary tools typically come in relatively inexpensive kits with a variety of bits

and shapers. You can use one of the grinding bits to clear away grout, and a grout-removal attachment to keep the bit centered in the seam. You can adjust the cutter to skim off a top layer of grout and prepare for regrouting, or use it at the full depth to carve away a grout seam and make it easy to remove adjacent tiles.

Setting Replacement Tile

Over floors, use a wood chisel to scrape and cut away any raised ribs of old adhesive. You don't have to remove all traces, but you do need to make room for a new layer of adhesive. Otherwise, the replacement tile will not embed enough to adhere properly, and may not set flush with the floor surface.

Over drywall, it's difficult to remove a tile without bringing along scraps of paper and some of the underlying gypsum. (Be sure to cut away any loose material using a utility knife before making a repair.)

On deep scars you can make a standard drywall patch with spackle, or simply set the new tile in a thick bed of adhesive. But if you apply a thick layer to fill drywall voids, you could push the tile below the wall surface, making it impossible to grout. So if you do take this shortcut, nestle the new tile in place and use masking tape to hold it flush with the surrounding wall surface.

Over any surface, work the new tile side to side to get a good bond, and leave it centered in the space to maintain even grout seams. Once the adhesive sets (usually overnight), you can add grout to finish the repair.

1. Drill holes using a masonry bit near the corners of the damaged tile. This helps to isolate the tile and prevents damage to the surrounding area.

2. You can slice along the edge of the tile using a utility knife if necessary, and then dig out the grout with a grout saw.

3. With the grout removed, it's easy to remove a cracked section of tile. Then you can use a cold chisel to lift and remove the remaining section.

4. To prepare the substrate, you need to scrape away any raised ribs of old adhesive that could prevent the new tile from seating.

5. Once the substrate is leveled, spread new tile adhesive using the end of a notched trowel, and set the replacement tile in position. You may need to butter the back of the replacement tile as well. If you were replacing a heavy item, such as a ceramic soap dish, keep the item in position by taping it to well-secured tiles using masking tape.

TILE TIP: To avoid damage to surrounding tiles during a repair, isolate a damaged tile by cutting through and digging out the grout.

1. Isolate the damaged tile by drilling holes in the surrounding grout joints. You may also need to score between the tiles using a utility knife.

2. Dig out the grout around the tile, starting in the corner and working your way along the seam using a narrow screwdriver or cold chisel.

3. Start the cut between the fixture and the trapped tile by scoring the surface. A glass cutter may help, but a cutting wheel works better.

4. Once the grout is removed and the fixture seam is scored (or cut through completely), you can break out the remaining sections of exposed tile.

5. Align a new tile on the grid next to the damaged area,

and transfer the fixture outline using a compass. You might use a contour gauge instead.

6. To create the cleanest possible cuts for the butt joints, use a wet saw wherever possible. Next best is a snap cutter and tile nippers.

7. Scrape old adhesive off the substrate to make way for the replacement. Then apply a ribbed bed of adhesive and set the new tile.

8. To seal the joints between the fixture and the new cut tile, add a thin bead of flexible, silicone-based caulk along the seams.

TILE TIP: To mark a glazed tile, use a grease pencil. A lead pencil won't transfer, and a pen can easily smudge.

Fixing Trapped Tiles

Tiles that crack in the middle of a floor are easy enough to replace. But the job becomes more difficult when part of the tile is trapped beneath a cabinet, sink, toilet, or other fixture that you can't or don't want to remove. Trapped-tile repairs can be tricky. But it's possible to make a repair that will look as though you replaced the entire tile without removing the fixture.

Start by clearing out the grout around the broken tile. Then score and carefully cut along the seam between the tile and the trapping fixture, and remove the exposed portion of the damaged tile. The next step is to mark and cut a replacement tile that will nestle against the fixture. You can mark the new tile by transferring the fixture outline with a contour gauge or a compass. Then cut the replacement on a wet saw, or use a snap cutter and tile nippers, as the shape requires.

Scrape the old adhesive off the substrate, apply a new ribbed layer of adhesive, and set the replacement. Use masking tape to secure it until the adhesive sets. Grout the tile, and caulk the exposed seam between the tile and fixture.

Where tiles butt against fixtures, you should apply a bead of flexible caulk to seal the seams.

glossary

Backer board Cement-based panel with a fiberglass-reinforced coating; used as underlayment for tile. Also called cementitious backer units, or CBUs.

Backsplash The tiled wall area behind a countertop, sink, or stove.

Battens Thin wood strips used to support ceramic tile and ensure straight courses.

Beating block A block of wood covered with carpet or other protective material, used in conjunction with a hammer to bed tiles into adhesive.

Bisque The clay body of a tile, or the clay from which the tile is made.

Bond coat A thin layer of adhesive applied over the substrate.

Bridging Crossbrace supports between floor joists used to reinforce the floor.

Bullnose tile A trim tile with one rounded edge, used to finish off outside corners.

Buttering Applying adhesive to the back of a tile.

Carborundum stone A coarse-grit, silicone-carbide whetstone used to smooth cut edges of ceramic tile. Also called a Crystolon or India stone.

Cleats Blocks used to support wood braces or other members.

Cold chisel A heavy, blunt-edged chisel used in masonry work, typically for chipping or breaking up brick, stone, concrete, ceramic tile, and other masonry materials.

Control joints Grooves cut into a concrete slab to confine cracking; cracks form along the joints rather than randomly across the slab.

Course A single row of tiles, usually runs horizontally.

Cove A trim or finishing tile that creates a smooth joint between adjacent walls, a wall and a floor, or other surfaces.

Cure The period of time that concrete, tile adhesive, or grout must be left in order for it to reach full strength.

Dry-set mortar A cement-based adhesive, so-called because it does not have to be kept constantly damp to cure.

Furring strip Narrow strips of wood attached to a surface to build it out. Provide nailing for underlayment panels.

Glass cutter A pencil-shaped metal tool, at one end of which is a wheel-shaped cutter used for scoring glass or glazed ceramic tile.

Grout A binder and filler applied in the joints between ceramic tile. Grouts may either be sanded (sand added) or unsanded.

Hearth A noncombustible horizontal surface in front of a fireplace; the hearth may be flush with the surrounding floor or raised above it.

Horizontal working lines Level, horizontal lines that serve as a guide for laying horizontal courses of tile on a wall or other vertical surface.

Isolation joint Flexible material inserted between two dissimilar floor or wall materials (concrete and wood, for example) to allow for different expansion rates.

Layout stick A straight, long, narrow stick marked in increments of tile widths and grout joints.

Lugs Nubs or projections formed into tile edges to maintain even spacing between tiles.

Mastic Common term used for organic-based adhesives.

Open time The amount of time adhesive can stay on a surface before it dries out and no longer forms an effective bond.

Organic adhesive A tile adhesive that contains volatile organic compounds or solvents; also referred to as mastic.

Plumb line A long string weighted at one end with a metal plumb bob, used to determine true vertical lines.

Porosity In tiling terms, the amount of water a ceramic tile will absorb.

Prime coat A sealer coat of adhesive or tile sealant that keeps the substrate from drawing moisture out of the tile adhesive.

Riser The vertical face of steps or stairs.

Rubber float A flat, rubber-faced tool used to apply grout.

Score To scratch or etch a cutline in a glazed tile, prior to cutting. The tile will snap or break along the scored line.

Sealer A liquid coating used to protect unglazed tiles and grout joints.

Shims Thin, wedge-shaped pieces of wood, such as cedar roof shingles, inserted in gaps between framing members to prevent movement or correct sagging.

Snap cutter A hand-operated tool used to make straight cuts in tiles.

Spacers Individually inserted lugs or plastic crosses of an even thickness, used to keep grout joints consistent between tiles.

Substrate The surface or underlayment to which tile is applied.

Step nosing An extruded aluminum strip with a vinyl insert, installed on the front edge of stair or step treads to provide traction and prevent slips.

Striking joints Shaping concave grout or mortar joints between tiles.

Stub walls Short or partial walls that form the opening in a shower enclosure.

Thick-bed mortar A thick layer of mortar (more than ½ inch) that is used for leveling an uneven surface for tiling.

Thinset adhesives Any cement-based or organic adhesive applied in a thin layer (less than ½ inch) for setting tile.

Tile nipper Plier-type tool used to make irregular shaped cuts in tile.

Tread The horizontal face of a step or stair structure.

Trim tiles Specially formed tiles that are used to finish off inside or outside edges and corners of tile installations.

Underlayment Smooth panels of plywood, hardboard, or backer board used as a base for setting tile or other surfacing materials.

Vertical working lines Marked lines based on plumb, true, verticals; used as guides for laying tile on a wall.

Waterproof membrane A polyethylene film (usually 4 mil thick) or tar paper installed to prevent moisture condensation or penetration. Also called a vapor barrier.

index

■ Adhesives, 17, 21–22, 61, 85
Antique tiles, 9
Aprons, 10
Art Deco tiles, 9
Arts and Crafts tiles, 9

■ Backer board, 84
Backsplash, 63, 72–77
Bases, 10
Base trim, removing, 52
Bathrooms, wall tiles in, 47
Beads, 10
Bridging, 34
Bullnose, 10
Byzantines, 7

■ Cabinets, strengthening, 64
Caulking gun, 19
Cement backer boards (CBUs), 20
Cement-based grouts, 22
Ceramic tiles, 7, 8, 9
  antique, 9
  characteristics of, 8
  color of, 25, 27
  cutting, 47, 61
  embedding and leveling, 18
  finish of, 26
  firing, 7, 8
  floor, 9
  glazing, 7, 8
  hand-painted, 9
  history of, 7
  impervious, 8
  irregular, 30
  modern, 7
  mosaic, 9
  nonvitreous, 8
  pattern of, 26, 30
  porosity of, 8
  removing, 79, 106
  replaced, 107–109
  selection of, 8–9
  setting replacement, 106
  shape of, 10, 11, 25, 30
  size of, 10, 11, 25
  stone, 7
  texture of, 25
  trim and specialty, 10
  vitreous, 8
  wall, 9
  wear resistance of, 7
Chalk-line box, 13
Clay, 7
Computer-aided (CAD) services, 48
Concrete

  tiling existing, 96–99
  tiling over, 36
Concrete floors, preparing, 37
Counter edging, 63
Counters, 64, 65
Countertops, 62–72
Coves, 10, 47
Cut tiles, dealing with, 28, 30
Cutting tools, 14–16

■ Delft tile, 7
Diagonal layouts, 39, 49
Drain fixtures, 83
Dry-set grout, 23
Dry-set mortars, 21
Drywall, 53–54, 56–57

■ Electrical box, extending, 50–51
Epoxy-based mortars, 22
Epoxy grout, 23

■ Field tiles, installing, 41
Finishing tools, 19
Fireplaces, 91–93
Fixtures, 79, 83
Floats, 17
Floor tiles, 9, 24–45
Framing square, 28

■ Glass cutter, 14
Glazed pavers, 9
Glazed tile, 9
Glazed tiles, 8
Goggles, 13
Grab bars, 88, 89
Greenboard, 84
Grout, 10, 22–23, 45
  applying, 44
  cleaning old, 102
  impact on design, 26
  removing old, 103, 106
  sealing, 22, 102
  types of, 23
Grout tools, 19
Guillotine cutter, 14

■ Hammer, 13
Hand-painted tiles, 9
Hard-water problems, 101
Hearth, 91, 92
Holes, patching small, in drywall,
  53–54

■ Jack-on-jack layouts, 49
Job site safety, 40
Joints, tooling and sealing, 44

■ Knee pads, 13, 28

■ Laser levels, 40
Latex portland cement grout, 23
Latex portland cement mortars, 21
Layout and prep tools, 13
Layout stick, making, 31
Level, checking for, 28, 29
L-shaped rooms, lines for, 39

■ Majolica tile, 7
Measuring tape, 13
Moisture, checking for, 36
Mortar, 21–22
Mortar-bed floor, installing, 83
Mosaic tiles, 7, 9
Mural tiles, 9

■ Offset measuring, 43
Organic mastic adhesives, 22
Out-of-square rooms, lines for, 38
Outside corners, repairing, 54, 55

■ Partial tiles, 42, 43
Pipe wrench, 13
Plaster, preparing and repairing, 54
Porous tiles, 8
Portland cement grout, 22
Portland cement mortars, 21
Prefab pans, installing, 80–81
Pregrouted tile panels, 10

■ Respirator, 13
Rounds, 10
Routine cleaning, 101
Running bond layouts, 49

■ Saddles, 44
Safety glasses, 13
Scale drawing, making, 28
Score-and-snap method, 14
Scribing to an uneven wall, 68
Sealers, 23
Sealing, 45
Setting tools and materials, 17–18
Shapes, cutting irregular, 16
Sheet-mounted tiles, 10
Shims, 34
Showers, 78–89

Glossary/Index

Shower seats, 88
Single tiles, 10
Sink cutouts, 66–67
Snap tile cutter, 14, 15, 61
Soap dishes, 88, 89
Specialty tiling, 90–91
Spirit level, 28
Square, checking for, 28, 29
Squeegee, 19
Stain removal, 101
Stairs, 94–95
Striking and jointing tools, 19
Subfloor, strengthening, 33, 34
Swimming-pool edging, 10

■ Thickset, 7, 21
Thinset, 7, 21, 79
3-4-5 triangle method, 28
Thresholds, 44
Tile nippers, 16
Tile spacers, 18
Tools, 13–19

Trowels, 17
Tubs, 78–89
Tub surrounds, 103, 104–105

■ Underlayment, 34–35
Unglazed tiles, sealing, 102

■ V-caps, 10

■ Walls, 9, 46–61
Water absorption, 8
Waxing, 102
Wet areas, walls in, 51
Wet saw, 14, 15
Windowsill trim, 10
Working lines, establishing
    for countertops, 68
    for floor tiles, 38–39
    for tub and shower tile, 84
    for wall tiles, 58–59

Photo Credits

Illustrations by: Robert LaPointe, Norman Nuding, James Randolph

All photography by John Parsekian/CH, unless noted otherwise.

page 1: Mark Lohman
page 3: *top* Jerry Pavia, design: Ed Schramm Tile Work, courtesy of the Wright Residence; *center* Jerry Pavia; *bottom* Mark Lohman
page 5: *top* Mark Samu, design: Lucianna Samu Design; *bottom both* Jerry Pavia, *left* courtesy of the Tuttle Residence
page 6: *top both* Mark Lohman; *bottom* Jerry Pavia, design: Gail Lyster Tile Work, courtesy of the Simms Residence
page 7: Jerry Pavia, design: Ed Schramm Tile Work, courtesy of the Wright Residence
page 8: courtesy of American Olean
page 9: *left* Brian Vanden Brink; *top center* courtesy of American Olean; *top right* courtesy of Abbate Tile; *bottom center* & *right* D/Dreamstime.com
page 24: *left* & *top right* courtesy of Armstrong; *right center* courtesy of Abbate Tile; *bottom right* Jerry Pavia, courtesy of the Tuttle Residence
page 25: courtesy of Abbate Tile
page 26: *top* Phillip H. Ennis; *bottom* Tony Giammarino/Giammarino & Dworkin, design: Kat Liebschwager
page 27: Peter Tata, design: Cindy Cook/ Interior Selections
page 32: courtesy of Abbate Tile
page 43: *right* courtesy of American Olean
page 46: *top left* Jerry Pavia, design: Ed Schramm Tile Work, courtesy of the Wright Residence; *top right* Jerry Pavia, design: Gail Lyster Tile Work, courtesy of the Taylor

Residence; *bottom right* Tony Giammarino/Giammarino & Dworkin, architect: Lisa Taranto; *bottom left* Mark Lohman
page 48: *all* courtesy of Maticad
page 49: *bottom* Mark Samu
page 51: courtesy of Dal-Tile
pages 53–55: *all* Merle Henkenius
page 62: *top left* Mark Lohman, design: Kathryne Design; *top right* & *bottom left* Jerry Pavia, design: Ed Schramm Tile Work, courtesy of the Wright Residence; *bottom right* Mark Lohman
page 77: *top* Tony Giammarino/Giammarino & Dworkin
page 78: *left* Tony Giammarino/Giammarino & Dworkin, architect: Lisa Taranto; *top right* Mark Lohman; *bottom right* Tony Giammarino/Giammarino & Dworkin, architect: Joe Yates
page 81: *top* Jerry Pavia, design: Tim Thomas Tile Work, courtesy of the Fredricksen Residence
page 84: Tria Giovan
page 85: courtesy of Dal-Tile
page 90: *top left* Mark Samu, design: Susan Fredman Design; *top center, top right* & *bottom all* Mark Lohman
page 91: courtesy of Tile Restoration Center
page 94: Mark Lohman
page 96: Tony Giammarino/Giammarino & Dworkin, design: gardenatriums.com
page 100: *top left* & *bottom* Mark Lohman; *top center* Tony Giammarino/Giammarino & Dworkin; *top right* Jerry Pavia, design: Ed Schramm Tile Work, courtesy of the Wright Residence
page 103: *top* Tony Giammarino/Giammarino & Dworkin
page 109: *bottom right* courtesy of Dal-Tile

Metric Conversion

Length		
1 inch	25.4 mm	
1 foot	0.3048 m	
1 yard	0.9144 m	
1 mile	1.61 km	

Area		
1 square inch	645 mm²	
1 square foot	0.0929 m²	
1 square yard	0.8361 m²	
1 acre	4046.86 m²	
1 square mile	2.59 km²	

Volume		
1 cubic inch	16.3870 cm³	
1 cubic foot	0.03 m³	
1 cubic yard	0.77 m³	

Common Lumber Equivalents

Sizes: Metric cross sections are so close to their U.S. sizes, as noted below, that for most purposes they may be considered equivalents.

Dimensional lumber	1 x 2	19 x 38 mm
	1 x 4	19 x 89 mm
	2 x 2	38 x 38 mm
	2 x 4	38 x 89 mm
	2 x 6	38 x 140 mm
	2 x 8	38 x 184 mm
	2 x 10	38 x 235 mm
	2 x 12	38 x 286 mm
Sheet sizes	4 x 8 ft.	1200 x 2400 mm
	4 x 10 ft.	1200 x 3000 mm
Sheet thicknesses	¼ in.	6 mm
	⅜ in.	9 mm
	½ in.	12 mm
	¾ in.	19 mm
Stud/joist spacing	16 in. o.c.	400 mm o.c.
	24 in. o.c.	600 mm o.c.

Capacity		
1 fluid ounce	29.57 mL	
1 pint	473.18 mL	
1 quart	1.14 L	
1 gallon	3.79 L	

Weight		
1 ounce	28.35g	
1 pound	0.45kg	

Temperature

Celsius = Fahrenheit – 32 x ⅝
Fahrenheit = Celsius x 1.8 + 32